The Traveling HERDING Teacher

by Bob Vest

as told to Kathleen Freeman Kelly

Copyright © 2014 by Kathleen Freeman Kelly.
All rights reserved.

ISBN 13: 978-1-939054-28-9
ISBN 10: 1-939054-28-1

No portion of this work may be used or reproduced in any manner whatsoever without written permission.

Photos courtesy of Rachel Vest.

The techniques taught in this book may or may not be right for your situation. If you choose to use these methods, you will hold the author, publisher, and all of it's representatives harmless.

Statements, opinions, and instructions expressed by the author are not necessarily those of the publisher and its affiliates. Neither shall be liable for erroneous information.

1 3 5 7 9 8 6 4 2

Printed in the United States of America

Published by

Rowe Publishing

www.rowepub.com
Stockton, Kansas

PREFACE

**In memory of
Robert Eugene "Bob" Vest
11/19/1937 – 7/11/2009**
The Traveling Herding Teacher

The Traveling Herding Teacher

This book was originally undertaken as a joint project but never finished. Following Bob's death, this manuscript lay silent for several years and I finally decided to undertake its completion as a tribute to and in memory of Bob Vest. Bob helped so many people over the years and it is an honor to have known him and worked with him. I hope this book will provide help and encouragement for those who remember Bob and those starting in herding who may never have had the pleasure of meeting him.

Here's to you, Bob!

CONTENTS

1	Introduction	1
2	What You Need to Know About Herding	7
3	The Concept of Mastery	28
4	For Those New to Herding	32
5	Building Interest	43
6	The Call Off	51
7	The Flanks	54
8	The Stop	66
9	The Back and Out	73
10	The Walk Up	78
11	The Look Back	87
12	Influencing the Eye of the Sheep	94
13	Introduction to Whistles	98
14	Trialing	103
15	The Outrun and Lift	111
16	The Fetch	126
17	The Drive	138
18	The Pen	146
19	Shed and Split	155
20	Introduction to Working Ducks and Cattle	172
21	Common Myths and Misconceptions About Herding	179
	How This Book Came About	187

INTRODUCTION

Who am I?

Let me introduce myself. My name is Bob Vest. I have worked with dogs and livestock and dog handlers for over 40 years. I have worked with a variety of breeds of dogs and types of stock (sheep, cattle, horses, and ducks). Hardly a day goes by that I do not work a dog or help someone else with their dog. I currently travel approximately 70,000 miles during a year and conduct approximately 200 days of clinics per year and numerous private lessons. I have trialed or currently compete in trials sanctioned by the American Kennel Club (AKC), Australian Shepherd Club of America (ASCA), United States Border Collie Handlers Association (USBCHA), and American Herding Breeds Association (AHBA), as well as cattle trials that are not affiliated with an organization. The last few years I have not had much time to trial because of my teaching and training schedule. I also have judged trials of all kinds (Border Collies, AKC, ASCA, AHBA, and Kelpies).

Why am I writing this book?

I am writing this book because many of my students have asked me to put my techniques in writing. They want to be able to use it as a reference and to help them remember what I've told them at clinics. I appreciate each and every one of the people and dogs that I've had an opportunity to help because I have learned something from each and every one of them. Each time I'm able to help someone, I also help myself to better understand the relationship between people and their dogs.

Rachel, my wife, has encouraged me to stop and answer all the questions she can ask. I take it for granted that people will do certain things. Rachel helps me realize that not everybody knows to do the things that I do automatically. She has helped me learn to break things down into little steps so they can learn what to do. She has encouraged me to develop a step-by-step process for teaching and learning and to recognize the components of each task or exercise, as presented in this book. She also gives up her time and unselfishly allows me to expend my time and energy helping others. She takes telephone calls, helps organize things, answers people's questions, and allows people to be part of our lives. I realize that I am blessed to have such a relationship. We are thankful and appreciative that we are able to share our lives, thoughts and knowledge with other people who love dogs and appreciate livestock as much as we do. Thank you, Rachel!

People Who Have Influenced Me

In addition to my wife, Rachel, who has been instrumental in my development and progress as a teacher and trainer, I have been influenced by a number of people over the years. I was lucky enough to live at a time when there were many people who were artists in training animals. I thank my father for instilling his belief that you can do anything if you try. He also taught me the value of being a perfectionist and setting high standards. When I was in the eighth grade my father told me that I never let my dogs be dogs. In other words, I was a control freak and had to control everything the dog did or he would not be perfect. He was telling me that I should allow the dog to be himself and that he would be a better dog than if I told him every thing he did!

Another person who really influenced me was Louis Pence. He never had a bad word to say about anyone else or their dog. He took the time to help me understand dogs and dog training. Sometimes it took me a long time to recognize the wisdom of his advice. There are two things in particular that he told me that still stand out in my mind. First, he told me that I needed to teach my dogs to 'hurry up and take their time.' In other words, the dogs needed to have several speeds and learn to hurry up and then to calm back down and take their time. The other was that you can't train a dog until he can control the livestock. This means that you can't begin training your dog until he has the ability to go around the stock and move the stock where you are walking. Don't try to train the dog before the dog can control his livestock.

Nyle Sealine is another person who has influenced me. He has been a good friend and shared his knowledge of dogs and sheep with me over the years. One of the most important things that he has taught me was to stand still when working my dog. I used to hop around like a Mexican jumping bean in a hot skillet! I was all over the place and so was my dog! So, Nyle came up behind me and held my arms so that I could not move. He made me stand perfectly still while I worked my dog. He showed me that the dog would quiet down and that I should not blame the dog for being rowdy when I was the one that was creating it! He has shared so many other things through our visits, that I need to say thank you to Nyle, his wife Caroline, and their family for sharing many years of joy and friendship. If you ever have the opportunity to interact with Nyle, I'm sure you will come to appreciate the knowledge that he has and that he loves to share with others.

Vern Thorpe and his wife, Susan, and their children have been a part of my life for many years. He has been like a brother to me and his children have been like my own. I have to thank Vern for helping me in working with livestock and never letting my feet float off the ground nor letting me sink so deep into the water that I drowned. If you get to thinking that you are better than you are, he'll bust your balloon and make sure that your feet stay on the ground. Likewise, if you are sinking, he will reach down and pull you up. It is a true friend who will honestly tell you how it is and keep you from fooling yourself or blaming others.

Bill Cockran is another gentleman who taught me about manners around the trail field. I had seen some sheep jump over a fence and run down to another field. Being young and cocky, I figured I would show off my dog and return the sheep. There I was bringing those sheep back, all the while whistling and hollering like a one-man band. In the meantime, another group of sheep had been set out for him and he was going around the trail course. He did not appreciate me showing back up with the other group of sheep in the middle of his run! He let me know about this in no uncertain terms. It took me several years to get over being mad and to finally thank him for teaching me about etiquette on the trial field. So, when somebody tells you something you don't want to hear, try to remember that it may be for your own good and that it may help you later in life.

Ben Mean and his wife also deserve mention. Ben has been a good friend and when it comes to working a dog on cattle, he has shared his ideas and thoughts and has taught me a lot about working cattle. If you are interested in learning more about cattle and working dogs on cattle, Ben is an excellent person to learn from. I want to thank Ben, Nyle and Vern for helping me to start the Australian Fund, a fund that helps bring a trainer and family over each year from Australia to share their thoughts and ideas with America. This annual event has been quite successful and has been a learning experience for all of us. People from all of the USA come together to help each other and learn. It has enabled us to get to know people from all over the USA and we have formed lasting friendships and relationships through this event.

I'd like to thank all of my friends in Australia who have shared their knowledge and methods of training. This includes John White and his wife and son, Gary; Chris Stapleton and his wife; and Greg Prince and his wife. There are countless other people who I have likely forgotten to mention. I hope to continue to have many years of friendship with each and every one of them.

I'd like to thank Kathy Kelly for spending hours motivating me to put my thoughts on paper and motivating me to write this book. She and Rachel finally convinced me that this would be a good project and for tricking me into coming to Scotland in order to get this started. Most everybody knows that I don't want to leave the USA. I've had a wonderful time visiting, working with her and her dogs and working on this book. I'd like to thank Smokey Gray and his wife, Anne, for their hospitality.

What is in this book?

This book is written for anybody who is interested in understanding more about herding and teaching and learning more about herding. This book will cover some of the concepts important for understanding herding. It will present what I consider to be the 8 basic tools for herding and how to teach these to your dog. In addition, it will cover the parts of the trial course as a way to illustrate the uses of these tools. The trial course will be important to those of you who wish to compete with your dogs, but can also provide a yardstick for evaluating the progress of and quality of your training.

Sheep are the type of livestock that will be used throughout this book; an introduction to other types of livestock is included, but not presented in detail. Perhaps additional books will be forthcoming on working cattle or ducks! An introduction to trialing is also included since herding competitions are becoming a popular and rewarding activity for many dogs and handlers.

What do I hope you will get out of this book?

I hope that this book will give you some tools to use in training your dog. I hope it will help you better understand your dog, whether you want to compete or use your dog on a working farm. Dogs have been part of my life and I want you to be able to improve your abilities as a handler and to improve your relationship with your dog. I would like you to be able to pick this book up after you have been to a clinic or lesson and refresh your memory. If it inspires you to progress in your training and helps you to better handle your dog and reach your own and your dog's potential, then I will be pleased.

I think the greatest satisfaction that any teacher can have is to have his students become better than he is! It is quite a complement to see your students out doing clinics themselves and that they are as good as your own. Using my method with addition of their own distinctions and personality is a great complement. When you start teaching is when you start learning! Each and every one of you has the ability to help somebody else! By helping somebody else you will also be helping yourself. Don't worry about what people say or what they think about you when you are helping others. The satisfaction of helping someone else is more important than the criticism of others who do not have the will or ability to give of themselves to help others. Thank you for honoring me by allowing me to work with you and your dog and by perpetuating the circle of learning by helping others.

Bob and Rachel Vest, a great team!

WHAT YOU NEED TO KNOW ABOUT HERDING

Basic Tools for Herding

There are 8 basic tools for herding around which all herding tasks and training are based.

8 Basic Tools for Herding
1. Interest
2. Call Off
3. Left and Right Flanks
4. Lie Down and Stand (Stop)
5. Out
6. Back
7. Walk Up
8. Look Back

These are the tools that you will need in herding. I will try to explain how to train your dog in order to have these tools to work with.

1. Interest

INTEREST refers to the desire of the dog to work stock. First and foremost, a stock dog must have the instinct and desire to work. Coupled with this should be the desire to work for and with you. The desire to work for and with you may make up for deficiencies of interest. But, even the most naturally talented dog with a strong desire, instinct and interest in working may be very frustrating if he lacks the desire to work for and with you. The dog that will work with you, but with less interest, may develop more interest as he finds he enjoys doing things for and with you. As he learns to work and gains confidence, his drive and keenness will develop. If your dog has little interest in working and/or little interest in working for and with you, herding will be very difficult. You will have to be persistent and provide the motivation for BOTH of you in order to work stock. It may take you longer to accomplish the training and herding tasks. But, if you are willing to put in the time and effort, it is possible to train to a certain level.

2. Call Off (That'll Do)

Once you have a dog with sufficient interest to work sheep, then you will need to be able to call him off! I usually let a dog drag a rope so that I can make sure I can catch him and enforce the command for calling off. Basic obedience training when not on stock will be of benefit in helping your dog learn to call off stock. The traditional call off command is THAT'LL DO.

3. Left and Right Flanks

These commands are to tell your dog to move clockwise or counterclockwise around the perimeter of the sheep. A flank is meant to have the dog move around the sheep, not to have the dog move the sheep. This is an important distinction when starting a dog! The traditional flanking commands are COME BY (move clockwise around the sheep) and AWAY TO ME (move counterclockwise around the sheep). These can be shortened or lengthened in order to create shorter or longer flanks or to decrease or increase the amount of movement you desire from the dog.

4. Lie and Stand Down (Stop)

LIE DOWN, STAND, or STOP are commands for stopping the dog. Having the ability to have the dog either lie down on command or stand on command is useful since there are some instances when a lie down is preferred and others when a stand is preferred. A lie down may be needed when a rapid stop or release of pressure is needed, while a stand may be preferred when continued contact and presence to influence the sheep is desired. It is easier for the dog to move forward and put pressure on the stock or to back off from the pressure or fall back and cover when he is on his feet compared to lying down.

5. Out

The OUT command tells the dog to give more room as he is moving around the sheep. He will move at a greater distance from the sheep while flanking. It also may be used to move the dog directly away from the stock without flanking.

6. Back

I use the BACK command to have the dog back up while facing the sheep. This way he does not turn away from the sheep, but increases his distance from them. This command is very useful when teaching the dog to make rounded or square flanks, when teaching the dog to pace his stock, and in reprimanding the dog for pushing too hard or cutting in on his flanks. It is helpful when working in tight places and in situations in which you may need to release the pressure on the stock in order to hold them or prior to flanking.

7. Walk Up

The WALK UP is used to get the dog to move straight toward the stock. Once set on this line the dog should continue to move the stock in the indicated direction. He should continue to walk the stock in the indicated direction until you ask him to change that direction or until he reaches an obstruction to movement of the stock (such as a fence).

8. Look Back

The LOOK BACK command is used to get a dog to look away from the sheep that he is currently controlling in order to go back and collect other sheep that were not included in the original group that he collected. This may include sheep that are out of sight.

In the chapters of this book, we will deal with teaching these tools to your dog. Virtually all of the steps in training and the exercises in this book are designed to teach or use these basic tools. Most problems that handlers encounter with their dogs while herding can be traced to problems with these 8 basic tools. By addressing the basics, providing a good foundation, and constantly returning to the basics in order to maintain a sound foundation, we can ensure that our dogs and ourselves consistently perform to a high standard. All tasks in herding represent refinements and combinations of these basic tools. By continuing to refine these tools and how you put them together, you will be able to develop an extensive repertoire of skills. This should include the ability to move rapidly or slowly, with great force or pressure or little force, or at a great distance or close at hand. The ability to control speed, direction and distance from the livestock has an almost infinite number of variations that provide the ultimate challenge to achieving the potential of the dog and handler, working together to perform a task or in competition.

Once the dog and handler have mastered the basics, they must then use these tools in a variety of situations in order to gain life experience. By exposing yourself and your dog to as many situations, types of livestock, types of terrain and other conditions as possible. Both you and the dog will learn to handle most any situation that will arise!

Other Concepts

In the Pocket

The 'pocket' is the place where the dog needs to be in order to move the stock to the place you want and in the manner you desire. If he comes out of the pocket, this will result in problems in keeping things smooth and the sheep will be more likely to deviate from where you would like them to be.

For instance, picture taking a balloon and blowing it up. Then, push a pencil eraser into the balloon. This will make the balloon move away from the pencil. The indentation of the pencil eraser is the pocket. If the dog is not pushing hard enough to make a slight pressure (corresponding to the indentation in the balloon), the sheep will not move or will not move in the direction or way you want. If the dog is pushing too hard, then the sheep will likely explode (just like the balloon). If the pressure from the pencil is constantly changing, the movement of the balloon becomes erratic. The same occurs with the sheep when the pressure from the dog is constantly changing or bouncing all over. With continued pressure the balloon's movement will speed up. But, its movement can only increase in speed to a certain degree. If the progress of the balloon is then stopped, the continued pressure will explode the balloon. Continued pressure of the dog when the sheep are stopped will result in a similar explosion—sheep will go everywhere!

The 'pocket' is the place where pressure is concentrated in order to get the results you want. You will want the dog to be in the pocket and to remain there because this will result in the most efficient and effective way to move his sheep. If the dog bounces out of the pocket or is constantly changing it will cause you more problems when moving your sheep.

The Hook

This expression refers to 2 things. It can refer to the dog being hooked onto the sheep—this is the placing and distance of the dog whereby he will influence the sheep. Picture the balloon that we used in the example above for 'in the pocket.' In this case, the balloon represents the sheep. The dog is represented by the hand that holds the pencil. The pencil represents the hook or connection between the dog and the sheep. Disconnection of the hook, maintenance of the hook or excessive pressure from the hook can all result, depending on the movement of the dog (your hand) or the sheep (the balloon).

Continuous maintenance of the hook with just the right amount of pressure from the balloon (sheep) and the hand holding the pencil (dog) results in the smoothest movement of the balloon. When this occurs between the dog and the sheep, it results in a continuous flow of the sheep that is a thing of beauty to watch! If the hook or connection is lost or wavers, the movement is much more erratic. If the hook is subjected to excessive pressure from the sheep or the dog, a disaster may be imminent!

You have to also consider the dog's ability to influence the eye of the sheep when he is hooked. This can be represented by a fine piece of wire that runs along the side of the balloon and is tied to the front of the balloon. It can either pull or push the front part of the balloon. If it pulls too hard on the front of the balloon (sheep), the balloon may be turned back. If it pushes too hard, the front of the balloon may deviate. If the pressure stays steady on both ends of the balloon (the pencil and the wire), then you can control the balloon (the sheep) and will be able to do more things with it. So, if you can get the dog hooked on the sheep and on the eye (hooked on both ends), you will be able to control both ends of the sheep!

Interest in Herding

Interest reflects a dog's desire to herd. Things that you should remember are:

Some dogs, regardless of the breed, will not herd.

Even though you may have a breed of dog that is considered to be a 'herding breed,' not all dogs will have sufficient instinct or interest to herd.

Some breeds and/or lines of dogs have been selected for certain characteristics over the years; these characteristics may NOT include herding instinct or ability. In some dogs herding instinct or interest in herding may develop with continued or repeated exposure to livestock and may be dependent on age and/or previous training. Some dogs may have had negative experiences that transfer to the herding situation and which prevent expression of the herding instinct.

There is a difference between herding instinct and the instinct to chase or prey on stock.

Many dogs will have some chase or prey-related instinct. Although herding instinct was developed through modification of the hunting instincts of early domesticated dogs, it differs from the chase or prey instinct alone. Herding instinct involves the desire to control and move livestock, but not the intent to cause harm that will be the result in chasing or preying on stock. For the inexperienced it may be difficult to determine the difference in these types of reactions. It may be difficult to recognize whether or not true herding instinct is present on the basis of a single or a few exposures to stock. In some breeds the initial manifestations of herding instinct may be strongly prey or chase oriented. However, with a bit of training and continued exposure, it may be possible to determine if sufficient herding instinct and desire to please the handler is present to work with.

Herding instinct may exist without natural ability in herding.

The presence of herding instinct alone does not indicate that the dog will be naturally talented with regarding to herding, keeping stock together or doing the tasks of herding. If sufficient herding instinct is present to keep the dog on the job, then the handler may need to learn to read stock extremely well in order to help the dog and make up for deficiencies in natural ability that may limit the ability of the dog to make progress in herding or to perform to a high standard that requires the ability of the dog to read the stock, be in the right place at the right time and to anticipate stock movements.

Important Factors When Herding

Pressure

Pressure is the amount of tension or force exerted or applied in a particular situation. Pressure may exist because of the sheep, the terrain, the handler or the dog. Each may exert pressures upon one another. The degree of pressure will vary, depending on the circumstances. Some examples that may help you understand pressures:

- Pressure is exerted between sheep when one group of sheep is trying to get to another group of sheep. Let's say that one group of sheep in the field is trying to get to or join another group of their buddies that are in another area of the field, in the barn or in a holding pen in another area. Should the dog try to control one group of sheep and keep them from joining with another the group of sheep, the dog will be subject to the pressure exerted by the sheep trying to get to their buddies. This may make the sheep extremely difficult to control or to move. Whereas, the same sheep, when out of sight or smell of other sheep, may be more easily handled and controlled by the dog.
- Pressure exerted by the handler on the sheep. If the sheep are afraid of the handler or not accustomed to being handled, they may feel pressure from the handler and will not spontaneously approach the handler. In this situation, the dog may be able to bring the sheep up to a certain distance from the handler (where they start to feel the pressure from the handler) and then may not be able to push the sheep any closer to the handler without having the sheep split, go in different directions or become more difficult to control.
- Pressure exerted by the dog on the sheep. Let's say the desired outcome is to have the sheep brought to the handler and to be held quietly in the area of the handler. If the dog does not realize the desired goal or is not trained to accomplish this, he may continue to exert pressure on the sheep as they near the handler, causing continued movement of the sheep and lack of quiet settling in the desired manner. This is particularly common with young dogs—they don't know how to relax pressure and allow sheep to settle when they have reached the handler. It almost always takes some training for young dogs to learn how to do this; in a few cases this will be part of their instinct and manifested with little or no training.

- Pressure exerted by the terrain on the sheep. Particularly in rough country there may be pressures exerted by the terrain on the sheep. They may prefer to pick a certain path along which to move rather than move in a direct, straight line toward the handler (which is desired in competitions and sometimes as the most efficient means of movement of stock in order to cover the shortest distance in the least amount of time). For instance, there may be ravines or dips through which sheep may not want to move either because of the steepness of the bank or because of natural paths along the side of a hill.

Balance

Dogs exhibit balance while fetching, driving, and penning. It is most commonly discussed with regard to fetching behavior, but is also very important while driving. It refers to the ability of the dog to:
- position himself relative to the sheep in order to get them to move in the desired direction (to get behind the sheep to fetch them or to be in a position to push them along the desired line of a drive or into a pen);
- keep the sheep together (also a function of power and the ability of the dog to see a big picture vs. focusing on a few individuals);
- ability to move the sheep to the handler in a straight line while fetching or in a straight line while driving and
- exert enough pressure to keep the sheep moving at the speed that the handler requires.

The handler is not the focus of balance. Balance relates to the place you want to take and sheep and how you take them there. With herding instinct, balance is most usually manifested as the desire of the dog to move around the sheep. He may balance on the heads of the sheep, wanting to stop or control the sheep movement or may balance by wanting to get behind the sheep and move them toward the handler. Many inexperienced dogs will not be refined in their exhibition of balance and will need practice in order to find and develop their balance.

The basic movement that reflects balance in many dogs at the early stages is manifested by the tendency of the dog to move away from the handler as the handler moves toward him and by the desire to keep the stock between the handler and himself. Some dogs, however, will be more comfortable moving one way around the stock (clockwise or counterclockwise). This is an important trait that needs to be recognized immediately in order to use the dog's more comfortable tendencies during the initial exposure and then to work on the less comfortable side as part of the development of a well-rounded dog that works easily on either side. This is like learning to become ambidextrous!

Movement and Control

The herding instinct is often manifested as the desire and ability to create and maintain movement in the stock. This may be exuberant movement that is not the controlled movement we aim for in the trained dog and may include running, biting (called gripping), circling around the stock and/or wearing (movement back and forth). All of these possibilities are linked to the dog's desire to control stock. Sometimes the dog will try to stop the movement of the stock by holding on a fence or in a corner or by constantly going to the heads and turning the sheep first one way and then the other. A very aggressive dog may sometimes take the sheep off their feet, holding them using its teeth and/or body to stop the movement and control the stock. This represents an extreme response that may be difficult to mold or train, but which does not automatically exclude a dog as a herding prospect.

So, there are a variety of dog behaviors that can indicate herding instinct. That is why it is so difficult for many inexperienced dogs and handlers to learn to cope with herding instinct and to mold it to achieve the desired degree of training, obedience and control while maintaining natural ability and thinking on the part of the dog. A true training challenge!

Power

Power in a dog can be manifested in many different ways. It reflects the presence and confidence of the dog and influences his ability to move livestock. A powerful dog will be able to move most all types of livestock. But, some stock, no matter what you do will be impossible to move!

The Powerful Dog

Some people think that power in a dog is the ability of the dog to bite (grip). However, a powerful dog will rarely, if ever, **have** to bite. When he does have to bite it is a correct bite—this means he bites on the nose or heels down low unless told to bite someplace else by the handler. He will walk up, will stand in the face of the sheep, even if the sheep butt at him.. He will not bite because there is no real threat to him. The sheep may look threatening, but the dog has the confidence and does not fear this sheep or the handler has told him that he does not want him to bite. Other times, the sheep will look the same, but the powerful dog will nip him on the nose and either stand or fall back to cover in order to keep the sheep where you want it to be.

To me, the person who is the most powerful is not the one that needs to strike out to justify their opinion; it is the person who can stand, keep a cool hand and take pressure from the opposition without becoming physical. The same goes for dogs! The powerful dog may change his posture to suit the situation—sometimes he may look directly at the sheep and 'puff himself up' to appear bigger. At other times he may look away from the sheep, acting meeker to the sheep so that he can move them without provoking a fight. Sometimes the dog will give ground, yet hold, in order to win the battle. When you see this in a dog you will appreciate his ability to read what is needed in that particular situation.

The Dog Without Power

The dog that grips is no different than the dog that gives ground or lies down when faced with a tough situation. Both dogs are reacting to the pressure, just in different ways. They are no different than people who exhibit different reactions when under pressure. Some people will get into the face of the other person, while others go into avoidance; some may eat or drink excessively. All of these things are attempts to relieve pressure. It should be no surprise that dogs also react differently under pressure. Some will eat grass or manure. Others will lie down or run away (avoidance). Some will jump up and get in your face. The ones I really like are the ones that react as if to say 'no big deal' and get on with life! You can help your dog develop confidence in himself and his ability by understanding why he does these things. You can put him in situations and help him to learn alternative ways to react. You can help desensitize him to those stimuli that previously caused an undesirable reaction (like a bite). You can use your voice, body language, commands and reminders to help prevent a bite, to help him relax, encourage him and to prevent development of problems.

If you have never reacted inappropriately to pressure you should appreciate the fact that you have blown your top, but then have gotten over it. If you can get over a bad situation, so can your dog. If you believe in your dog, he'll believe in you. If you have confidence in your dog and do not hold a grudge regarding his previous reactions and transgressions, it will be easier to help him improve. Dogs do not scheme or plan to do things wrong. They do not commit premeditated acts of violence. They just react to pressure at the time.

You can teach a dog that wants to grip or which lacks power the tools that he will need to become more powerful. By teaching him to change his posture and to nip on command you can help him develop the confidence he needs to become a powerful presence. You can help him change his posture by encouragement and motivation. You can help him have some success and then will not have to help him as much the next time. An observer of this dog will never know that he was not born a powerful dog!

Training Aids

Training aids can be a cane, a bamboo pole, a piece of PCV pipe, a whip, a bag, a rolled up plastic feed sack, a hog paddle, a rake, a crook, a rope or any other object that people use to help them to get the dog to do something.

Selection of training aids that you will use will depend on what you find the easiest to work with and who is helping you learn about herding. Different trainers will have training aids that will be their favorites for working young or older dogs. A training aid may help you teach your dog to stop or move around the sheep or may help you move the sheep. When you first start training a dog, you will emphasize the message you are communicating to the dog by using your training aid a lot. As your training progresses, you should start using it less and less until the dog will respond quickly to your verbal or whistle commands without the training aid. At any time, you may need to use a training aid to help you enforce a command or to reinforce basic aspects that need to be practiced or polished. A training aid is only an extension of your arm and your authority. The dog should respect it but not fear it. Any aid may become a crutch if you begin to rely on it too much.

One way to help your dog become accustomed to a training aid and learn that he should not fear it, is to pat the dog with it and run it over his body. He will learn that it can be associated with pleasure, as well as to provide a correction. If the dog is pushing over the training aid, he is not respecting it. Maybe you did not use the aid correctly, maybe you need to use your body language in conjunction with it. Watching experienced trainers use their training aids will be important in you forming a mental picture that will help you also use these aids.

Once the dog has responded to your training aid, you will need to make sure that you do not continue to exert pressure with it. If you are constantly pushing on the dog with your training aid, the dog will never get any relief that shows him he is doing well and responded correctly. He will likely start to lose respect for it. Learning to use your body in conjunction with the training aid is a large part of learning to train your dog. Use your training aid as a block more than a punishment. It is to help convince the dog to do something, not to force the dog to do something. By blocking the dog, you are making it difficult for him to do those things that you don't want him to do. By using the training aid you are also making it easier for him to do those things that you want him to do. This philosophy and approach to training will result in a better attitude in the dog (and also in the handler!) than using the training aid to FORCE a dog to do something. Your dog will begin to resent you and to resent herding if you constantly force him to be in a situation that makes him uncomfortable. Part of your job as a handler and trainer is to provide opportunities for your dog to feel comfortable with herding and to use these opportunities to help him understand what you want him to do.

Teaching Sheep to Tie

Other things which can be considered training aids include pens or enclosures within which sheep can be held in order to set up a training situation or provide a particular type of work or exercise. Another thing, which can be helpful, is teaching your sheep to be tied up. This is helpful in setting up particular training situations and in assuring that sheep will stay in one place when you need them to. This will help your dog learn more quickly and to provide a clear message for your dog.

To teach your sheep to tie, you will start with a single sheep. You can use a dog collar around the neck of the sheep and tie him up to a strong post or fence that he cannot pull down. Tie him up short enough (with approximately 1 foot of rope) that he cannot get tangled in the rope. You may tie him up when you feed him so that he will enjoy being tied. Do not leave him tied without supervision. At first he may fight being tied and pull against the rope. Leave him to figure out that he cannot get away and that giving in to being tied is easier than fighting. I will leave the collar on him when I turn him lose so that I can easily identify the sheep with which I have been working and so that I can easily catch him. Once he is comfortable being tied, I will lead the sheep around with a leash or rope tied to the collar. This is a good opportunity to teach your dog to walk along quietly behind the sheep. Do not let your dog harass the sheep while you are leading it. The presence of a well behaved dog may make this much easier. I usually want to have at least 2 sheep that are broke to tie. Once I have two individuals that are properly acclimatized, I will take them out and tie them to a stake..

I have two different kinds of stakes. One of the stakes is a swivel stake that allows the sheep to move around. The other is a release stake; with it you can pull a pin and release the sheep if you need this for a particular exercise. I will use the swivel stake to tie sheep out when teaching outruns, the look back and some flanks. I use the release stake for outruns and look backs because it is easy to release the sheep if I want to reward the dog for doing these correctly. These are quite useful for people who have trouble keeping their sheep where they need them to be. However, it should be used only for brief periods and with sheep that have been acclimatized to its use.

I will also teach the sheep to tie along a fence with a flank strap. In addition to tying the head to a post on the fence, I will put a flank strap around him and tie it to the fence. This will keep him from being able to swing around. You can accomplish the same thing by putting a panel up alongside the tied sheep to prevent him from swinging around. I find that this works very well.

I use a sheep tied to a fence with a flank strap or a side panel for teaching a dog to walk up on the sheep, to teach the dog to nip on command and for dogs that lack confidence walking up to the head of the sheep. See the Chapters on Teaching the Walk Up, Shed and Split and Teaching the Look Back for more exercises and details using tied sheep.

Teaching Your Dog to Walk Behind You

It is important to teach your dog to walk behind you instead of pulling or pushing out in front of you. Behind means that the dog's head will not cross in front of an imaginary line drawn out from your shoulders. He should literally be at your heels and not lagging way behind you or way out to the side. This teaches the dog to wait for you to ask him to move through gates or a door and to wait for you to ask him to go to work. When the dog runs out in front of you, he is already half way to the sheep and thinking about going to work; he has taken charge of the situation without you asking him to and he is more likely to be thinking about what he wants to do than what you want him to do. This will also be helpful when walking to the post at a trial. By positioning him behind you and to the side the you want him to outrun, you will be establishing a pattern that will help him learn to outrun to the side on which he is walking, help him learn to look for his sheep up the field and help him learn to wait for you to ask him to go to work.

To get your dog to do this, you will have to practice walking him while away from sheep first and on a leash. I start this after the dog has learned to lead. I usually put the leash in my hand behind my back and start walking. I will carry a small switch or stick that is 3' to 4' long and the small end no bigger than my smallest finger. It is not meant to hurt the dog, but only to irritate him. If the dog starts to go past, I'll reach over and tap him on the front part of his leg and say 'behind.' You can put different words on this to indicate whether you want him on your right or left side, or just pat your leg to indicate the side once he is behind you.

After he begins to respond with my hand holding the leash behind me, I'll walk with my hand at my side, but still expect the dog to stay in the correct position. Finally, I will work on this with him dragging the leash. You should be able to call him from playing and put him behind you without picking up the leash when he fully understands this.

If the dog does not pay attention to your switch and continues to pull ahead of you or periodically dart out in front, consider whether you may be swinging the switch or using your body to block the dog so that he is not truly learning this command. The idea not to keep him from making the mistake of going out in front of you, but to let the mistake happen so that you can correct it and show him what you want him to do. If you have threatened him with the switch, but not actually tapped him on the front legs, he will learn to disregard the switch.

If you try to do this with a lot of slack in the leash, the dog will learn to get out around you. Keep the leash short so you do not have to reach for him. If you need to, you can use your stick to reach across in front and around to his far side and 'tuck' him back in behind and beside you.

Be careful that you do not get after your dog too severely or drill your dog excessively on this at one session, because he may then be too shy of the switch and will drag behind you. He may be afraid to work the stock or be afraid of your crook or training aid. If you have to use it for a correction, use it, forget it and move on. A light tap is more effective than a swat. If you will tap him lightly he will begin to respond to the stick; if you swat him he is more likely to learn to fear the stick. As with all corrections and training, the degree of pressure you put on the dog should be appropriate for that dog, what the dog is doing (going only a short distance ahead versus lunging enthusiastically ahead) and the situation.

You will want to have your dog able to walk out in front of you, off to the side or behind you. So, make sure that you practice these things, particularly when they are young puppies. You shouldn't always make the dog walk behind you, but should be able to make him walk behind you when you ask him to. If you never allow the dog to walk out in front of you, it may be difficult to teach him to WALK UP when on stock.

Another good idea is to have a release word. This can be any word you choose, but should indicate that it is okay for him to go and play and that you are no longer asking for his attention or work. This is different from THAT'LL DO which indicates that he should no longer work stock and is primarily used when away from the stock.

Philosophy of Training

My philosophy of training is based on learning to work with the dog and learning to understand what he is thinking and what it takes for me to show the dog what I want him to do with the least amount of pressure and discomfort on his part and my own. I have to learn to read a variety of signs that the dog produces—to determine if he understands, if he is confused, or if he is unsure or uncomfortable. If you see your dog becoming uncomfortable, you may have to do something else and come back to working on the problem area at a later time. The better the trainer, the better he understands the dog's potential and when to ask and when not to ask things of him. Sometimes you have to wait a long time for the right moment to ask him to do a particular thing. You may have to wait for the opportunity to get the correct response. Many opportunities will present themselves during training. Dogs learn from consistent work (how you ask him, the way you asked him and the body language you use in conjunction with this) and repetition.

For example, you can ask the dog to lie down in many different places. If you concentrate on the lie down and not the places. He will learn to stop, no matter where he is or what else is happening. You can work many different types of sheep, but I am interested in teaching him to stop, regardless of what the sheep are doing. When he will consistently do this, he will now be ready to move on to something else because you now have an initial piece from which you can start building. You can't start building until the dog shows you what he is comfortable doing. You may have to start working with Z with one dog, while another dog will need to start with A. Both dogs will need to learn the alphabet, but will be starting from different places. In the end, both will know the alphabet, but may have taken different paths to get there!

I believe that once the dog starts learning, he will continue to learn. Once he learns how to learn he will develop a thirst for knowledge. If the dog is trying he is never wrong—he just didn't get it quite right!

You may have to repeat an exercise 300 times with one dog and 3 times with another in order to get a desired response. But, both dogs will learn the same things at the end of the day. If you look at a dog only with regard for those things that he is doing wrong, this will often result in the dog continuing to do things wrong. If you can recognize what he is doing well it may be possible to make progress based on this response or reaction.

When you are working your dog, you have to believe that the dog can do it, that you can do it and that you and your dog can do it together. If you will be persistent, keep your sights on your goals and believe in yourself and your dog, you will be able to accomplish many things. But, you will have to work at it. Herding requires hours of practice and repetition in order to achieve a high standard of work. It is one of the most challenging activities that you can undertake in partnership with your dog, but is also one of the most rewarding and fascinating.

Paradigms for Herding

There are several ideas that I have found help people understand certain parts of herding, the herding dog mentality and approach to training. These paradigms or comparisons include the *55 gallon drum*, a thing I call *the hook* and a thing I call *staying in the pocket*.

The 55-Gallon Drum

This is a way that I look at a dog, his potential and your relationship with him as a trainer. Let's say that you have 3 different dogs, each represented by a 55-gallon drum. The first dog has a full drum with 55 gallons of confidence. The second dog has 25 gallons of confidence and the third dog has only 10 gallons of confidence. Let's say that the trainer of the first dog (55 gallons of confidence), has a negative attitude and negative approach. He shouts at the dog, gets after the dog when the dog is right, ignores the dog when he is wrong and is inconsistent with his commands. He physically punishes the dog and seldom, if ever, pats his dog or lets him know that he is his friend. The dog is trying the best he can, but may not always get things right since he has not had good training opportunities. A little over 0.3 of a gallon of confidence disappears out of this dog every time he is worked.

The trainer of the second dog (25 gallons of confidence) takes the dog out and works it. The dog does everything he asks, but the trainer has never asked the dog to try challenging things. The dog would be willing and able to undertake these challenges, if asked, and showed what to do. But, the trainer just goes along and expects the dog to find his own path. He never takes any confidence out, but does not build any confidence to add to the dog.

The third dog (10 gallons of confidence) has a trainer who believes in him. His trainer helps show him that he can do many different things. He helps the dog learn to do things and allows the dog some freedom to figure out how to do it himself, but never allows him to fail. If the dog has trouble he will continue to help the dog until he understands how to do it. He enjoys having the dog with him and spends time with him. The dog and the trainer enjoy each other and are friends. They become a good team. This trainer adds a little over 0.3 of a gallon of confidence to this dog each time he works this dog.

After 6 months (180 days) of training, the first dog becomes empty of all confidence and belief in himself. All of his confidence has been destroyed and wasted. The dog is empty of all confidence. Because he cannot do anything, he becomes homeless. The second dog has stayed in the same place; he and his trainer are happy with each other and enjoy what they do. But, they do not challenge themselves and so do not achieve their true potential. They complain that they have bad luck or no luck at all.

The third dog, however, now has confidence that is running over the top of the barrel. He has made great strides in his training and his relationship with his trainer. Everyone wishes they had a dog like him because he has everything that anyone would ever want. They no longer see the dog that started with 10 gallons of confidence. They only see what he is today and do not think about all that has gone into him. They figure he has been that way all of his life. This is why a little belief, helping your dog, and challenging yourself and your dog to be the best that you can be will be rewarding.

So, the next time you train your dog, think about the 55-gallon drum!

Polishing Your Dog

This is a paradigm about training. Picture a piece of rock in the side of the hill. You want to take this rock and make a statue. You will start out with dynamite to blast away this rock until you have a piece of approximately the right size. You may have to take a jackhammer to break it away from the surrounding rock. Now you will have to use a grinder and a sandblaster to shape the rock, but it still has a very rough surface. As you continue over many days, you will use finer and finer sandpaper to smooth the rock. Eventually you will be using polish and a buffing compound to bring it to a high gloss. There is, however, a single spot that is harder than the rest of the stone and which will not smooth out. You want to be careful about polishing this spot because it gets that part of the rock very hot and may create a permanent blemish. If you keep polishing a little over a long time it will gradually smooth out and the entire rock will be gleaming and polished. This is kind of like dog training! If you have a young dog, everything he does may be like the rock that is being blown out of the side of the hill with dynamite. As he progresses in his training, he is being hammered and chiseled. As he begins to understand things and masters his basics, this corresponds to the grinding with coarse materials that will begin to smooth the rock. As he goes on with his training that you will begin to recognize the areas that are harder than the rest of the rock. If you are not careful, you may spend too much time and apply too much pressure in trying to make these hard areas perfect. If you do this, they may become a permanent blemish. If you may have polished only a little bit a time and spent more time on other things, the harder areas would eventually have become polished without leaving a permanent blemish.

Correcting Your Dog

The best way to communicate with your dog is to wait until his head is toward you. If his tail is toward you, he may think you want him to run away. If the side of the dog is toward you, he will learn to go around you and avoid you. So, it is best to correct your dog or try to help your dog understand what you want when you are face-to-face with him. That way he can see what you want!

These 3 things (the 55-gallon drum, polishing the rock and correcting your dog) are my 3 favorite ways of providing parallels for dog training that help my perspective and vision with regard to training dogs. I hope they will help you do the same!

THE CONCEPT OF MASTERY

Introduction

In teaching scores of students, I've found a wide variety of approaches to learning and the *mastery* of skills and exercises. Many students seem to feel that 'understanding' or 'familiarity' with a task or exercise is sufficient and want to move on to what they consider 'more advanced' or 'more relevant' work without truly **mastering** the exercises.

Only through mastery of the basics can a sound foundation be built for progression to different stages of work. When the order of the exercises in this book is important, I will try to emphasize this and indicate the sequence that achieves the best results for most pupils. Sometimes it may be difficult to see the relevance of some aspects of work to others; I will try to make the exercises as relevant as possible to the final task or skill. Even the most skilled handlers and dogs constantly need to review and check up on the basics to make sure that no bad habits have crept in and that skills are practiced in a way that promotes a sound foundation for work, trialing and/or training.

Just running a course or working on the aspects needed for a trial or a particular working situation does not necessarily produce the foundation that is optimal for it! Think about the best football coaches—they do not have their players practicing by playing whole games or even portions of games every day. They work on basic skills that translate into the ability to play the game!

While practice in mastering the course and various aspects of the course is important for inexperienced handlers, it may not always be the best thing for the dog! Achieving a balance between the necessary practice of handling skills, course practice and training with the correct attitude of the dog and handler is the ultimate goal.

The details, exercises and foundation skills described in this book are meant to help you understand the concepts and to help you envision how the exercises should be done when applied correctly. The necessary practice and daily attention to training is up to you! There may be an extended period during which you may not be able to accomplish the exercise with the degree of accuracy and expertise you desire. But, if some degree of improvement can be achieved and you persist in your attempts to achieve the skills you will likely be successful! Too often I hear of handlers who, when they try a particular approach or exercise a few times and do not achieve rapid success, they conclude that 'that doesn't work with my dog' or 'that doesn't work for me' and give up. A certain amount of trust is required; not all exercises will work for all dogs or handlers. If you trust the teacher and have had success in the past with his/her techniques, do not be quick to give up with those things in which you do not have rapid success!

I offer my training techniques and experiences to you as an experienced stockperson and teacher. I hope that my efforts will enable you to become a Master of those aspects of herding that you wish to learn and that they will enhance your relationship with your dog and with livestock.

The Concept of Polish and Finishing a Dog

No dog or dog/handler team is ever truly finished training. No dog or handler is perfect, and each requires practice or refining of skills that may become defective through disuse (lack of opportunity to train, practice or use in everyday work) or ragged from conditions of work that require a job to be done without regard for the correctness of the skill (everyday work, trials, work with exceptionally rough stock, work with non-dog-broke stock, or work that does not rebuild the dog's confidence and refresh his natural tendencies and abilities).

In addition, remember that it is a natural part of dog behavior for the dog to periodically challenge the handler. This may be the result of asking the dog to do things that go against his natural instincts or may be because the dog does not always understand the reasons for what we ask him to do. We may lose or erode the trust of the dog when we ask him to do things that go against his natural instincts and take away part of his confidence and natural ability when we do not allow him to use it. This trust and natural ability need to be constantly checked and rebuilt in order to maintain a working relationship between the dog and handler that results in a high level partnership and accomplishment of sophisticated and complex tasks.

With polishing of skills needed for highly specialized tasks or trial work, it may be difficult to maintain the underlying base. Think of the example of polishing a rock to a high gloss. Initially it is rough and uneven. In the polishing you are wearing away the roughness, first using a rough material. This corresponds to the initial stages of training with polishing of the roughest parts of the dog. As you continue to polish the rock, you will use finer material and it will take less pressure to polish it. This corresponds to increasing precision and accuracy in the dog. When you get to this point with a stone or rock, you will begin using a buffing compound that will be less abrasive, but polish the stone and bring out the shine. The buffing compound for the dog is to allow the dog to work without interrupting his thoughts and provision of praise to let him know when he is right.

Now you get down to the very final polishing of the stone; you have to be careful not to polish in one spot too long and create a small area of imperfection or damage. With the dog you might have one thing that he is not as good at as you would like—be careful to polish the whole dog, not just concentrating on the one spot that may become burned and a permanent imperfection. Through allowing a small amount of imperfection, the whole dog will become perfected with time. Polish the whole dog, not just spots!

Concluding Remarks

To become a MASTER of anything is a long process. It is possible to do this much more quickly these days since there are many people who are very good at herding and have a lot to offer. You can visit with, watch and learn from many people and take the best from each one to make these things your own. As you continue to work, you will realize that none of us will every truly master every aspect of herding, but will be able to have the satisfaction of knowing that you are very good at what you do. A true master learns throughout life. Consider learning about herding and herding dogs as a life-time journey. When you begin thinking that you know everything, that is when you have quit wanting to learn!

Bob training Gator on sheep

FOR THOSE NEW TO HERDING

Introduction

If you have never worked with a herding dog before, consider buying an experienced dog of the breed in which you are interested or of a traditional herding breed such as a Border Collie. By having a trained dog, you will be able to learn how to handle and train without the uncertainty of also having an inexperienced dog! But, buying an experienced dog may be outside of the scope of some handlers or may not be considered by some who wish to work with a particular dog or dog breed. Realize that your inexperience may be limiting in terms of the progress you will make with your dog or may promote bad habits in a dog. But, with diligent practice and desire to learn, a high level of performance of dog and handler/trainer can be achieved!

For those inexperienced with herding, regardless of whether you are working with a trained dog or an inexperienced dog, it will be beneficial to obtain some help from an experienced handler and teacher. Ideally this person will have experience with the breed of dog you have to work with and will be interested in and experienced in teaching inexperienced handlers. Good teachers are hard to come by, but are invaluable in helping inexperienced persons learn about handling and training! Training and handling philosophies differ greatly, so you will want to gather as much information as you can about the possible trainer/teacher and may want to go and observe a training session before enrolling in one yourself. There are many accomplished trainers and teachers who give clinics nation-wide on a regular or by-arrangement basis. Clinics provide an opportunity for many people and dogs to have an introduction to herding, determine if their dog has suitable instinct and motivation to herd and to observe other people and dogs in action. The success of clinics and level of satisfaction of those attending clinics often depends on the venue, the facilities, the suitability of the livestock, and the level of experience of the attending handlers. Private lessons may be more expensive than clinics at which you share the instructor's time and expertise but may be useful at particular stages of training and learning. Even the most experienced handlers and trainers benefit from constructive criticism and discussion about techniques, styles and methods of training, application of commands and corrections and other facets of herding.

The initial aspects of training may be physically strenuous and require quick movement on the part of the handler in order to be in the right place at the right time. Sometimes sheep or inexperienced dogs are unpredictable, even when the best conditions and training facilities are utilized, so it is not without risk to handlers who may have bad knees or whose physical status may not withstand a hard knock from sheep or dog in an excited moment. During the initial and subsequent phases of training, considerable walking and/or running may be needed in some cases. If you have seen herding programs on television or videos where the handler is standing primarily in one spot (by a post in competition) and directing the dog, remember that you are seeing a highly trained dog and handler combination! THE STEPS TO ACHIEVING THIS STAGE OF EXPERTISE MAY REQUIRE CONSIDERABLY DIFFERENT SKILLS.

If there is an experienced trainer of your breed, you may consider sending your dog to that trainer for several days to several months to acquire some exposure. But, if you have a breed or individual that is very devoted to you (a one-person dog) or which does not show strong interest or instinct in stock, you may need to work with this dog yourself. Or, you may prefer to work with your dog yourself, either because of the cost of outside training, absence of availability of suitable training or because this is your personal preference. Realize that it may take you (an inexperienced handler/trainer) much longer to accomplish some aspects of training and that bad habits may develop because of your inexperience. However, you may be able to achieve a high level of personal satisfaction in working with a dog new to herding and learn many aspects or handling and training if you wish to attempt this. You will have to learn how to recognize and correct the bad habits that you may introduce during the learning process as a handler new to herding in order to keep from making the same mistakes or instilling this same habit in your subsequent dogs.

This is an important part of continuing to learn as you train subsequent dogs. Don't worry about making mistakes—this is just part of the training and learning process and it happens to everyone!

Experienced trainers and those with particular types of dogs may not feel that special facilities or stock are needed in order to work with inexperienced dogs. However, for the majority of people new to herding or those inexperienced in working with dogs new to herding, I have found that certain aspects of stock, facilities and equipment should be considered in order to achieve a high probability of initial success and satisfaction with the process. I usually recommend the following:

Tame Sheep

It is helpful to have at least 5-10 dog-broke sheep, accustomed to being handled by people and accustomed to being worked by dogs. If acclimatized by a knowledgeable individual, these sheep will be accustomed to going to or toward the handler, knowing that the handler is their protector from the inexperienced dog, and will usually respond reasonably, without excessive panic. It is almost impossible for an inexperienced handler and inexperienced dog to successfully tame sheep! Later you will need to introduce your dog to many different types of sheep, but tame, dog-broke sheep are essential for starting out.

Many people prefer a slightly smaller sheep for training, if available, since they may be physically more maneuverable and less heavy if they do happen to bump into you or crowd you because of an enthusiastic inexperienced dog. I have seen a variety of types of breeds of sheep used for training and almost any breed, if suitably acclimatized, may be used. However, some of the heavier breeds of sheep may become sour more easily and will be less beneficial for training at that stage. But, at the early stages of training, err on the side of caution—very dog-broke, tame sheep are needed by most people!

Ducks can be used effectively to start some types of dogs or to provide initial exposure with young puppies (no training, just exposure to stock), but are less inclined to be people-oriented, may bring out strong prey behavior in some dogs and may be more difficult for inexperienced handlers in an initial training situation. Therefore, sheep are my choice for starting dogs. If the dog is to work ducks and/or cattle, introduction to these types of stock can occur slightly later in training.

Suitable Facilities

My preference is to start inexperienced dogs in a confined area so that sheep, dog and handler can be controlled. An oval or rectangular pen of approximately 60' x 100' is a good size to consider for most types of dogs. If you are having trouble controlling your dog in this area, you may need to reduce the size of the pen to the point where you can be successful. It should be sturdily constructed with closely spaced posts that are well anchored, woven wire and/or wooden slats that prevent dogs or stock from sticking their heads through the fence or getting caught. The entire enclosure should be sturdy and should only have spaces that are small enough to prevent animals from escaping or getting caught.

Suitable Equipment

I usually recommend that inexperienced dogs and handlers start off with a rope attached to the dog's collar. The collar should be a buckle-collar that can be tightened so that the dog cannot slip out of it. The rope should be approximately 15' long and of suitable weight and strength according to the size of the dog. It provides a means to catch or control a dog, should it be needed. Shorter ropes may be used at different stages of training or the rope can be removed if the dog feels restrained or is sufficiently controllable and able to be caught without it. Most dogs will learn to drag a lightweight rope or line while working and will not be too worried by it.

Other Equipment

Other equipment may include a **crook**, a small broom with soft bristles or a **small plastic rake** (kiddie rake) with blunt plastic tines. A dog food bag (usually coated paper) or sometimes even hats or other things may be used to make noise, intimidate a dog slightly or provide correction during training. Some trainers use buggy whips with certain types of dogs (usually those sensitive to noise correction). All training tools may be used incorrectly or with poor results! All are meant to be **aids** or **tools** that help us more effectively communicate with our dogs, provide extensions of our arms or body, or provide physical barriers to dogs and/or stock. Don't become dependent on a particular training tool. I will try to explain the use of these tools in different situations as they arise in different places in this book.

Objectives for Starting a Dog on Stock

My primary and secondary objectives when starting a dog on stock are listed on the next page.

These may appear like simple things, but because the herding instinct is strong and you are dealing with a variety of factors, a dog and livestock, it may not always be easy to accomplish.

You cannot learn to assess these things from the pages of a book. Hopefully, this book will help you better understand herding and training for your dog and yourself. But, nothing beats having the opinion of an expert when you are unsure of what is happening or what direction to take.

Attendance at clinics or private lessons with a herding professional can be extremely beneficial. Experienced people may not always be good teachers, but all will likely have things that you can learn from.

Primary Objectives for Starting a Dog on Stock

1. Encourage manifestation of and development of herding instinct and interest in the dog in order for the dog to have an enjoyable first experience on stock.

2. Protect the livestock so that it is not hurt in the process.

3. Protect the dog so that he is not hurt in the process.

4. Instruct and manage the handler so that he/she is not hurt in the process.

Secondary Objectives for Starting a Dog on Stock

1. Determine the dog's natural tendencies and likely tendencies in order to effectively manage subsequent training sessions.

2. Determine the handler's ability to read stock and the dog and the handler's natural tendencies when put in a herding situation. This will help me determine how they can best be managed in future sessions and what they should be reminded of or what may be more or less difficult for them compared to other people.

3. Determine a program for the next few lessons that will likely fit the dog and handler combination.

The best combination is an experienced herding trainer who is also a good teacher! Approach your herding experiences with an open mind and willingness to listen and learn. There are advantages to exposure to a variety of persons and approaches, but consistency in instruction is also important. If you find someone whose style of herding and training fits with you and your dog's personality, it will likely be beneficial to follow the same lines of training over a long period of time rather than repeatedly changing based on snapshot evaluations by a variety of trainers. By periodically working with the same person, he/she will be able to get to know you and your dog, assess progress over time and help you with a long term training plan that will help you achieve your goals and attain a high level of satisfaction with your training process.

Recommendations for Starting a Dog on Stock

Many experienced trainers will size up a variety of factors in an inexperienced dog and adjust rapidly to these factors, producing a picture that makes it look easy. Don't forget, they had to start at the beginning when they were learning, too! Don't worry if things seem a blur to you during some initial lessons. Try to concentrate, watch and learn from others so that you can mentally see what's happening as it occurs with you and your dog. First you must be able to see it in others. Then you will be able to see it in yourself. Think about how you will respond to a particular situation in order to make progress with your own handling.

In order to take things step-by-step and anticipate what an individual dog's behavior will be on stock, I usually recommend first taking a dog to tame sheep in a small enclosure. I usually start out with the dog on a line, walking around the periphery of the pen or enclosure, watching to see whether he looks at the stock, wants to go directly to them or is anxious about the whole situation.

By walking the dog around the outside of the stock you are intentionally showing the dog the path you'd like him to take. You are also promoting a calm attitude. This will help both the dog and handler become comfortable around the sheep. For aggressive or excited dogs, modification of the attitude is important. You will have to prevent the dog from pulling you around the periphery of the pen and/or lunging to try to get to the sheep. I usually do not do much harsh correction at the first exposure, but will try to get this under control during the first several times the dog is taken to sheep. It may be of benefit to have an accomplished handler work with your dog or actively move around in the pen with you and your dog during the initial exposures in order to promote the type of movement and responses that will encourage the dog yet protect the livestock.

Common reactions that I see are:

Dog is slightly interested, but may sniff and eat sheep manure.

The dog may watch the sheep and then turn away. It is usually obvious that this type of dog will not intentionally do damage to the stock, so it is safe to let him take the next step and have some contact with the stock.

I would recommend having a friend hold this dog by the lead. Position yourself near to the tame sheep and sufficiently off the fence so that the dog will not feel intimidated by the fence as he is going around or behind the sheep. In a small area with a strange dog, this may require pulling the tame sheep toward you by a collar around their neck if they will not naturally come to you in the center of the pen.

Then have the holder let the dog go, initially dragging the line. See if the dog will naturally go around the sheep. You may have to step slightly to one side to encourage the dog to move around the sheep. For example, if you are facing the dog and are between the dog and the sheep, with your back to the sheep: step slightly to your left and extend your left arm out to the side to block movement of the dog to the left. This should result in movement of the dog in a clockwise direction around the sheep.

If the dog will not go around the sheep initially, you may turn your back on the dog and begin walking around the sheep or around the pen with the sheep following you. This may create some interest in the dog and initiate contact between the dog and the sheep. Once the dog starts moving toward the sheep you may then be able to stop and let him go around. In some cases, just getting the dog to follow the sheep as you walk around the pen will be sufficient progress for an initial exposure.

Some people have a tendency to point with their arm in the direction they want the dog to go. This should be avoided for several reasons:
1. It goes against the natural movement of the dog to move past or into an extended arm.
2. It may encourage the dog to watch the handler for signals rather than watching and reading the sheep, as we would desire.

For dogs that are doubtful or which need encouragement to approach the sheep, touching the sheep or patting them may be of benefit. For Shelties, puppies or small dogs, introducing the dog to sheep restrained in a very small pen, lifting them up onto the backs of tame sheep and generally letting them have a good sniff while on top of the sheep may help their confidence. For some dogs going up to the sheep on foot may be intimidating at first.

The dog is moderately aggressive and wants to really get to the stock.

This type of dog may not be comfortable with himself or the livestock. I may spend quite a lot of time walking this dog around the stock or walking toward the sheep, stopping and allowing them to move off. I will keep this dog from pulling me toward the stock or lunging at them. The aggressiveness of this type of dog usually reflects a lack of confidence in himself and his ability to move or control sheep. Once he has settled, I will let him go around the sheep while dragging the lead. I will try to keep the sheep between myself and the dog. If I see panic arising in this dog or a tendency to grip, I will try to stop the dog and restart him in the opposite direction around the stock. This may break the panic and uncertainty cycle that is promoting aggression. The objective is to keep his mind occupied while moving around the sheep. He should not be moving toward the sheep. He should become comfortable flanking around them, without the panic of moving forward.

I will not try to hold the dog off, but will actually invite him to come in to the sheep! If I try to hold the dog off, I will only contribute to the pressure on the dog and will likely cause a grip or bite. I will watch his reaction when I invite him in to the stock. If he moves forward aggressively I can be ready to discourage this action. The biggest tendency I see is for people to try to discourage this type of dog when he is only 'thinking about' coming forward aggressively to the stock; only when he is actually coming forward aggressively can you make the correction. This is the only way that he will understand that this type of movement is not acceptable.

The dog wants to go around the stock but does not show undue aggression.

This is the type of dog we would all like to have! This is a dog that has interest and instinct, but does not exhibit aggressive tendencies. Often this dog will want to please and work with the handler, but may not know how to do so without additional training. Many times this type of dog will easily go around the stock. If you step away from the stock too quickly, allowing this type of dog to come in to the stock before it is ready to do so, this may encourage this type of dog to grip or rush the sheep. The movement of the handler draws the dog into the sheep. With this type of dog it is important to determine that the dog stays the same distance from the sheep as he goes around and does not come into the sheep. Flanking the dog without moving stock will usually allow this type of dog to settle. After they have settled and quit thinking about moving forward onto the sheep, they will be receptive to small movements of the handler and quiet control of the sheep.

Concluding Remarks

There are many small subtleties with each starting dog that you can learn to recognize with continued practice and observation. For the inexperienced handler, help from a professional in starting your dog is highly recommended! Once the initial stages have been worked through and a degree of control established, with ability to call off and stop the dog, many inexperienced handlers and dogs are at a point where they can begin to work as a team and learn about herding.

Bob training Mick on sheep

BUILDING INTEREST

Introduction

Keen dogs that are eager to work may not need encouragement to build interest. However, with young puppies or dogs that may be reluctant to work stock, building their interest is important.

I will outline what I do with puppies and then with older dogs to introduce them to livestock and build interest.

Starting Young Puppies

If I am starting out with one or more puppies, I will first take them to ducks at approximately 8 weeks of age. I will have 2-3 ducks in an enclosed area (my duck pen is approximately 20' x 40'). I will set one or several puppies down in the pen and then I will move the ducks up and down the opposite long side of the pen. I will be observing the pups while doing this. I will expect to see one or more of them watching the ducks. At this age they may or may not do any more than this. I would like to see puppies looking at the ducks at this age, but with some breeds or individuals it may require several exposure sessions before they may show interest in the ducks. After several minutes, I will remove the puppies from the pen. They are never in the duck pen without supervision or for more than a few minutes at a time. I will take them to the ducks once a week when they are between 8 and 12 weeks of age.

Usually there is a progressive building of interest with repeated exposures. The puppies may show interest by trying to stop the ducks as I move them along one side of the pen or by running into the midst of the ducks. If a puppy runs into the midst of the ducks, I'll just set a plastic rake down between the duck and the puppy to make it difficult for the puppy to come into the ducks. I will not force the puppy, but this will enable him to figure out how to go around the ducks. They may try to go over or around the rake; you may have to move it in order to prevent this. Be patient and give the puppy time to figure out that there is another way to get around to the other side of the ducks. He will be learning to think for himself and figure out how to do things. This is an important skill for the puppy to develop and you will not be discouraging him in any way. I will repeat the exposures on a weekly basis until a puppy shows enough interest to approach and go around the ducks by himself (without having the other puppies with him).

Once a puppy has shown this level of interest, I will put this puppy in by himself, not with other puppies. I will do the same thing with the puppy by himself. I will try to position myself so that the puppy will cause the ducks to move toward me. This is the very beginning of teaching the puppy to fetch! I will not be putting any words or commands to movements at this time or trying to stop the puppy. I want him to learn to rate and move the stock at his own pace. In order to call the puppy off, I'll block him with a rake. If the puppy is hard to catch, I'll let him drag a short length of rope. I will use THAT'LL DO to bring him off the stock and then pet and play with him to show him that coming with me is a great place to be!

I'll do this up to about 6-8 months old. By this time I will be able to call him off. I will then start putting a stop on him. I do this by blocking the puppy as he goes around the ducks. If he tries to go one way or the other I'll block him again. Soon he will stop and look at me and I'll tell him the word for that I have chosen for stop/stand. I will not have him stopped for long. As soon as he pauses or stops for a very short time, I'll step to one side (eliminating the block) and let him go around the ducks. Be very careful that you do not stop your dog too often at this age! I continue to work the puppies approximately once a week until they are 10-12 months old. By doing this, you will have puppies that are fetching, stopping, moving off your body language and calling off. Since they have all these pieces in place, it will not take you long to teach them the words for their left and right flanks.

This seems to work very well for loose-eyed dogs within which you need to create and build interest in working stock. It may not be as important for dogs with more eye, but is not detrimental to their progress.

Developing Interest in Puppies While Away from Stock

There are some things that you can do to develop interest in herding with your pup if you do not have regular access to stock. You can use a mop, a broom or a stick with a rag tied to the end. Move the stick-rag/mop/broom across the floor in front of the pup and see if he will watch or try to herd the object. Vary the way that you move it. If the pup shows interest, try to get him to follow the object as you move it around in different ways. This interest in movement, trying to stop the movement or follow it are manifestations of herding instinct.

These things are best not overdone or done in conjunction with periodic exposure to livestock. If practiced too frequently or without exposure to stock they may result in the dog becoming 'fixated' on the object that you are using or paying more attention to you than to livestock when you actually take him to stock.

Developing the Work Ethic in Your Puppy

How you work with and socialize your puppy will affect the work ethic that your puppy develops. You will have to ask more of your dog as he matures. A good work ethic will include him being calm and relaxed as you ask him to go to work.

I commonly see people talking to a puppy from one side of a fence or enclosure. The puppy gets excited and whines or jumps up. Some people will encourage this. This begins to teach puppies habits that you may not be as pleased about in an older dog. I prefer to have people pick up my puppies and play with them, not just to talk to them from one side of the fence. They should begin to develop manners so that they sit while you are patting them. When I am walking my puppies on leash and people ask if they can pat or play with the puppy, I have the people come to the puppy and do not allow the puppy to go to them. I will have the puppy stand or sit as the people approach them and do not allow the puppy to lie down. This helps the puppy develop confidence when people are approaching him. In a crowd the puppy should not be sniffing, searching or trying to go to other people. The same goes for other dogs. My puppy or dog should not invade another dog's or person's space. This requires that you teach your puppy some manners. As the puppy matures, you will be asking them to do more. With your guidance and training, your dog will begin to know that there is a time to play and a time to work. If he has never been asked to work, to contain himself or to refrain from doing only what he wants to do at the time, when you ask him to do something and expect it to happen, he will be more likely to let you down. Herding training will require that your dog has a work ethic in order to advance to higher levels. Development of this work ethic will depend, in large part, on what you have done with your dog as a puppy and young dog.

Starting the Young Dog at 10-18 Months

If you have a young dog of 10-18 months that has not been to stock and which you would like to start, this is what I recommend.

At this age I would expect that you have taught your puppy to walk on a leash without pulling, to lie down and stay and to come to you. It really helps if you have an opportunity to take a young dog with you to the barn or around livestock. You may need to have the dog on a leash if it will not stay with you. You don't want to have to discourage him from wanting to work stock at this stage.

If you have not had your dog around stock prior to 10-12 months of age, he will likely be pulling and wanting to get at the stock and may be more panicked by movement of the stock in his presence. I would keep him on leash until he becomes comfortable around the stock. Do not turn him loose until you have a controlled situation.

Some experienced trainers will be able to start dogs in an open field. But, for beginning handlers and dogs I prefer to start in an oval or rectangular pen of approximately 60' x 100'. As described in Chapter 4, the enclosure should be escape-proof and sturdy. Three or four tame, dog-broke sheep are needed.

I start by walking the dog around the periphery of the pen until he is relaxed. If the dog is pulling or darting toward the sheep you may need to block his progress by putting a training aid (rake, crook, broom, bag, buggy whip) in front of him to block him and keep him beside you. The sheep should be in the center of the pen. I will position the dog so that I am to the inside of the pen and he is between me and the fence. Once he is relaxed and comfortable walking beside me around the pen, I may turn and walk toward the sheep with him and then stop and get him to stand quietly. If he is doing this well, I may move a short distance to one side or the other and call him to me (still on leash). This is the beginning of the CALL OFF.

Once he will do these things, then I am ready to let loose of the rope and help him move around the sheep and to move the sheep towards me. I stop the dog, step to the front of him with the rope in my hand. I step back from the dog; if he comes toward me, I step into him and stop him and cause him to step away from me. I will repeat this until the dog stops coming forward toward me. Once he will do this, I can drop the rope and step to one side and allow him to go around the sheep.

If he splits the sheep, you will have to block him and make sure he goes around the periphery of the sheep. This is why it is important to only start with a few sheep that will stay together—they will be less likely to split.

Once he is going around the sheep, you will be able to walk from side to side of the pen, without stopping. Once he is able to keep the sheep to you while you are walking around the pen, you will be ready to start teaching him to stop and to tuck the sheep in behind you when you stop a short distance away from the fence. You will stop and let the sheep go between you and the fence. If the dog wants to come into or around the sheep, you will block him. He will often turn and try to go around the sheep the other way—block him again. After several attempts and blocking, the dog will often stop and stand on his own. This is when you will start telling him the word you have chosen for stand/stop. Only use this command when you see that the dog is ready to stop. Do not keep repeating this command while the dog is on the move—this will just teach him to ignore the command. At this point I will also begin putting words/commands for flanking directions and the CALL OFF.

Starting Dogs 18 Months or Older

When starting a dog of 18 months or older, you may be dealing with a individual that is more mature physically and mentally and more set in their ways. You will have to work harder to ensure that you are part of the picture when they are working. This age dog will likely want to do more 'on his own' and consider you to be an interruption of his fun. It may take more time walking around, teaching the dog to give to your body pressure and step away from you than with a young dog. By making sure you have this foundation, it is more likely that they will respond to the pressure that you want to put on them.

Getting the Dog to Step Off of You

The dog has to respect your space in order for this to occur. You will have to put enough pressure to get the dog to give and step away from you. Once the dog steps away from you, you will also step back to relieve the pressure on him. If you continually put pressure on him he will be more likely to develop a bad attitude or try to escape that pressure by going around or toward you, rather than giving ground and stepping away from you. In order to get the dog to step away from you, you will need to move directly into his face. You may need to use a training aid (crook, rake, bag, etc.) to encourage them to move away from you and discourage forward movement (see Chapter, Teaching the Back and Out). This is a very useful command for pushy dogs and can be used at many stages of training to help maneuver the dog so that he understands what you want him to do. Until a dog will respond to the pressure of the handler, it will be impossible to make much progress and a fight to keep him off the stock is likely. I prefer to spend a little time developing this facet and not to fight!

Some dogs in this age group will easily go around the stock and stay off without a fight. You will be able to work them in the same way as described for puppies. I recommend taking these dogs to stock daily or as often as you can, but only for short sessions (usually 5-10 minutes at most).

Some dogs in this age group may not have much desire or they may be reluctant to leave your side. You may have to help this type of dog realize that it is okay to work stock. He may go to the stock, then return to the handler. The biggest problem with this type of dog is that handlers may try to force the dog to work or excite the dog by telling them to 'get them.' They may become even more concerned and anxious and may be less inclined to leave the handler and work the stock. Do not make a big deal out of it. With repeated exposures and gentle encouragement many dogs that are initially reluctant will gain interest and realize that it is okay to work the stock. Using a shhh-shh sound is sometimes helpful since it usually does not resemble any other command the dog may have heard. Another good thing to try is to turn this type of dog loose and then you go out and move the stock around yourself, ignoring the dog. It may take several exposures with you moving the stock around before he begins to participate.

Once he is wanting to do things, I will try to create a job that has a definite purpose and beginning, middle and end. This provides motivation for the dog and helps him see that there is a purpose to his participation. An easy way to do this is to move sheep from one pen to another or from a pen to their pasture or barn. He will have to help you take the sheep from the pen, through the gate, across a small distance to the next gate and then through that gate. Once they have been put into the new area, make sure that you call the dog off and make a fuss over him—give him some attention to let him know that he has done a great job. Walk back through the pen, stop him while you open the gate, walk him through and stop him. Then walk toward your sheep without encouraging him to go around the stock. Repeat the process of taking the sheep from one pen or place to another. One day you will find that he will go through the gate and want to run around the stock and bring them to the gate. This is exactly what you want him to do! Don't yell at him or say anything. If he splits the stock and tries to bring one or two to the gate, don't allow him to go through the gate. Don't get excited. He will likely soon look and see that there are several remaining sheep and will go get them. As his interest and desire increase, then you can begin to ask more of the dog and put some commands to his work. If you see his interest flag, you may have to go back and rebuild this interest as described above.

Concluding Remarks

Time and patience are important in building a dog's interest. Frequent and repeated exposure to stock with short sessions provide the optimal stimulation to build interest.

THE CALL OFF

Introduction

The CALL OFF is one of the first things I teach, as presented in the Chapter on Building Interest. It is important that you be able to call your dog off the sheep. The command that I use for the CALL OFF is 'THAT'LL DO'. This means for the dog to come off of the sheep; the job is finished and I don't want him to work any more when he hears this command. A fault that a lot of people make is to say 'that'll do' to call the dog toward them in order to make the dog flank. This can be used occasionally when you are unsure about a situation, but should not become a habit! In addition, this command, when used properly, will break the dog's concentration on the sheep, which is undesirable when flanking.

Teaching the Call Off

The foundation for this command is started when your puppy is young and you teach him to come to you. By letting a young pup drag a cord, it is easy to teach him to come to you by stepping on the cord, giving it a slight jerk and calling his name. This ensures that he will not be able to ignore the command and that he comes to you immediately when called. For calling a puppy or a young dog to you when off stock, I use 'here' or 'come' (not 'That'll do'). The 'That'll do' command is taught in the presence of stock and can be linked with the 'here' that he already knows to help him learn to come all the way back to you when he hears 'that'll do.' I may use 'here' or 'come' in conjunction with a flank instead of 'that'll do' during the early stages of training flanks. But, remember that he should respond to the flank command and not just to the 'here' command followed by the flank command. At some point he will be in a position where the 'here' is not going to be appropriate or helpful and he must still learn to take the desired flank command.

To teach the dog the meaning of 'that'll do,' have him on a rope and walk around and through the sheep, as you would to teach him to be calm in their presence. Walk toward the sheep with the dog and then stop and call him off, turning and walking away from the sheep as you do this. Practice this until the dog will readily respond without a jerk or reminder from the line. Then let him drag the line; you can step on the line so that if he fails to come when you say 'that'll do' you can pick up the line and give it a jerk to remind him to stop concentrating on the stock and come to you.

By this time you will likely have your dog moving around stock and doing some short fetches to you. Be sure to call the dog off several times during your work and not just when you are finished with your training session. As part of your work, flank the dog around the sheep, stop him on the opposite side of the sheep. Then walk through the sheep, toward and past the dog, stepping on the rope as you go by. Then call him off as you walk by him. Take him a short distance away and then put him back to work without delay. This will keep him happy about calling off and coming with you since it does not necessarily mean that working stock (his fun) is at an end. Later you will be able to call your dog off from any position relative to the sheep or in any phase of his work. He should be able to come by the sheep on the call off without forgetting himself and going back to work.

Then you will remove the rope. At this point the dog will become responsible for accepting and taking your command. You have taught him the meaning and enforced it with your training aid (the rope). Now, if he does not take the command, which you KNOW he knows and understands, you will have to exert some force and pressure in order to get him to come off of the stock and to you.

Prepare to be challenged at various times. Most dogs will choose to continue to work sheep at some point when you have called them off. You will then have to enforce your command by going to get him, getting between him and the stock or whatever it takes to get him to come to you. You will need to use whatever force or pressure is necessary to accomplish this and assert your authority, but be sure that you do not use excessive force or pressure in this correction. If you do not enforce this command you will be missing an important building block and you will not likely have the respect of the dog that you will need in order to make additional progress!

Problems with the CALL OFF

A word of caution: do not always drive the sheep away from you, stop the dog and then call him off. This may cause him to look back at you when you stop him while driving or may cause him to become reluctant to come off the stock. It is okay to sometimes call him off while driving, as long as you do not stop him first—call him off while he is moving. Or, flank him around or to one side of the stock and call him off when he is beside or on the opposite side of the sheep. He should not come through the sheep when he is called off from the opposite side of the sheep, but should go around them on one side or the other and then come directly to you. Be sure to pet him and make a fuss over him when he comes to you. It should be a pleasure. You have to be more exciting at this moment than the sheep are!

If the dog starts to come back to you and pauses or then wants to back to working the sheep without coming all the way to you, it is sometimes helpful for you to turn and move away from the dog. He will have to hurry to catch up with you. This situation will often arise when the dog is coming back to you but the movement of the sheep will catch his eye and make him think about returning to work.

THE FLANKS

Introduction

Flanks are the tools that you use to direct your dog to go left and right around the sheep. You can choose any words you want for flanks, but I use the traditional commands of COME BY and AWAY TO ME. I believe that if there were better commands that they would have been replaced by now!

COME BY or COME BY ME is used to have the dog go clockwise around the sheep. A good way to remember this is that the dog COMES BY the hands of the clock. If you want to shorten this flank (have the dog only move a short distance), you can use COME or BY.

AWAY TO ME is used to have the dog go counterclockwise around the sheep. This is AWAY from the way that the clock goes! If you want to shorten this flank, you can use AWAY or 'WAY.

There are two kinds of flanks based on the position of the dog relative to the sheep and handler: inside flanks and outside flanks. An outside flank is when the dog moves in an arc around the stock with you between him and the stock, leaves your side to go around the stock or flanks on the opposite side of the stock from the handler. An inside flank is when the dog is flanking while located between you and the sheep.

There are two kinds of flanks based on the distance that you want the dog to go on the flank. These are short flanks and long flanks. You will communicate the distance of the flank that you want by shortening or lengthening the command or by drawing out or shortening the words or whistles that you use for the command. The speed with which he moves while taking the flank can also be varied by the urgency of the command, repetition of the abbreviated command and loudness of the command.

These variations can be communicated to your dog in order to tell him the direction, speed, and length of the flank that you want.

Square flank refers to a flank that occurs when a dog turns at a right angle from a straight path toward the sheep in order to start off on his flank. There are some situations where a square flank is desirable and some in which a more rounded flank is best.

Teaching the Flanks

Initially you will use your body language to make your dog go in a particular direction around the sheep. I use a small plastic rake as a training aid to help my dogs learn to flank. It provides a wide surface that is easily visible to the dog. I can slide the rake directly at the dog in order to get him to lean backwards. At the point the dog thinks about turning or going backwards, I will turn the rake on its side so that it catches the dog's eye and he will turn away from it. This starts the dog on a nice rounded path to move around the sheep. You can use a pole or crook or other tools, but the rake is a good tool to use.

Once your dog shows interest in the stock, you will begin blocking him to prevent movement in one direction or the other. If the dog will not move around the stock in one direction, you may have to pick up the leash/rope and walk around the stock in the desired direction in order for him to become comfortable.

I'd like to be able to get a puppy or young dog to go left and right around the stock as soon as I can because all dogs have a particular direction at which they will be better. You can usually tell the uncomfortable side by way the dog reacts. He may not want to go one direction at all or may start to go this direction and then turn and go the other way. Other dogs may end up in the middle of their sheep or may run tighter on the uncomfortable side. Some dogs may flatten out on part of the flank on the uncomfortable side. If there is a problem which occurs only on one side and not on the other, it is likely because he is uncomfortable going this direction. It is like being right or left-handed for a person. So, if I can identify the weaker side, I can work more on it in order for the dog to be equally comfortable going in each direction. I will ask him to flank 2 or 3 times to the side at which he is less comfortable for each time that I flank him to his good side.

I find that most dogs will begin to get better because they are using both sides of their body. However, once in a while you will find a dog that just doesn't seem to get better on the poor side. When you ask him to flank he cuts in. No matter what you do, one side stays bad. When this happens, the dog is often on the wrong lead on that side—in other words, the front leg with which the dog leads or steps out the farthest is on the outside rather than the inside. To be correct, the dog should lead with the inside leg. The hind legs follow the same pattern as the front legs. If the dog is on the wrong lead, the inside leg is making a shorter path than the outside leg. Because the outside leg is making the longer stride, this makes it very hard for him to turn out. This affects your flanks and outruns, which is just a long flank. Sometimes you will have to back him up and slide the rake toward him to put his weight on his hind legs, then turn it over to get him to turn into the correct lead for that direction. By having him back up and then put his weight on his hind legs, he is more likely to be in position to lift himself up and naturally develop the correct lead. You may have to repeat this several times, but many dogs will learn rapidly to take the correct lead. If the dog has had an injury that is contributing to taking the wrong lead, it may be harder to correct. Notice how you move—many people will always start moving with the same leg. This should give you some insight into your dog's habits, as well as your own!

I have tried pushing out dogs on the flank with which they are uncomfortable, but have found that this is not nearly as successful as working with them to get the correct lead. As soon as they are consistently picking up the correct lead their flanking will begin to smooth out and become more correct.

I like a nice round flank that keeps the dog at the same circumference as he goes around his sheep without coming into the stock as he is flanking. As handlers we contribute to the tendency of the dog to fall in or come toward his stock as he is flanking if we start moving too early—for instance, if we start moving back as the dog passes the 9 or 3 o'clock position, we may encourage him to cut in or flatten out between 9 or 3 and 12 o'clock since he is now following his stock instead of staying out on the path that would complete a nice, rounded flank. I like to wait until the dog 'arrives' near 12 o'clock before stepping back so that the dog learns to complete his flank around the stock before he begins moving the stock. Otherwise, he is starting movement of the sheep before he completes his flank. This is one of the most common things that I see in dogs flanking—they are initiating movement of the sheep before they complete their flanks. The two things that most commonly cause it are:
1. stepping away too quickly, or
2. the dog is on the wrong lead.

As I am flanking the dog around me and the sheep I will make sure that the dog will come past me. I like to flank the dog at least 1.0 (360 degrees)—1.5 times around (540 degrees) so that he will be comfortable moving past me and not flip back to go the opposite direction when he feels the pressure of coming by me. I find that if you will turn with the dog, following at the level of his hip and keeping your shoulders perpendicular to the dog (so that you are not facing the dog), that this will help make him more comfortable. Later he should flank and move past you, regardless of your body positioning.

Square Flanks

To teach a square flank I have found that one of the best ways to get a dog to turn at the correct 90 degree angle is to have him back up just before I give him the flank. This will cause him to shift his weight to his hind end and turn off at a 90 degree angle. Another way to help your dog learn to make square flanks is to walk past the dog and slightly behind him before flanking him around you (Diagram 1). This will cause him to turn slightly off his sheep at slightly more than a right angle as he starts his flank. If he squares off to start and then cuts back in toward the sheep, you may need to stop him, walk across in front of him and then slightly behind and to the side and start him again. This can be repeated multiple times in order as the dog flanks in a large circle around the sheep in order to reinforce this command.

You can couple this with an OUT command to reinforce the OUT command in combination with the flank.

Flanking and Stopping Off Balance

Once you have your dog so that you can flank him left and right, have him fetch stock and walk up, it is time to teach him that you can stop him and have him walk up at any place on his flank that you want. Up until this time he has stopped opposite to the handler in order to bring the stock toward the handler. This is called 'stopping on balance.' When we stop the dog at any position other than that which would result in movement of stock toward the handler when he walks up, this is called 'stopping off balance.'

Pushing Sheep Off the Handler

In order to teach stopping and flanking off balance, I first need to teach the dog to walk up and push the stock past me. To do this, I will flank the dog around the stock and stop him. I will ask him to 'walk up.' As he pushes the sheep past me I will pick up his rope. I will use the rope to keep him from sliding around the stock and bringing them back to me. Then I walk forward with him, allowing him to walk out in front of me and push the sheep ahead for 3-4 feet. I only want to go a short distance at this point. Sometimes I will call him off (that'll do) and then repeat the exercise. Or, I may back him up, flank him around and then repeat it or tell him to OUT and then flank and repeat the exercise. I will practice this until he is comfortable doing this and I do not need to pick up the rope to keep him from breaking around

Diagram 1

Teaching Square Flanks

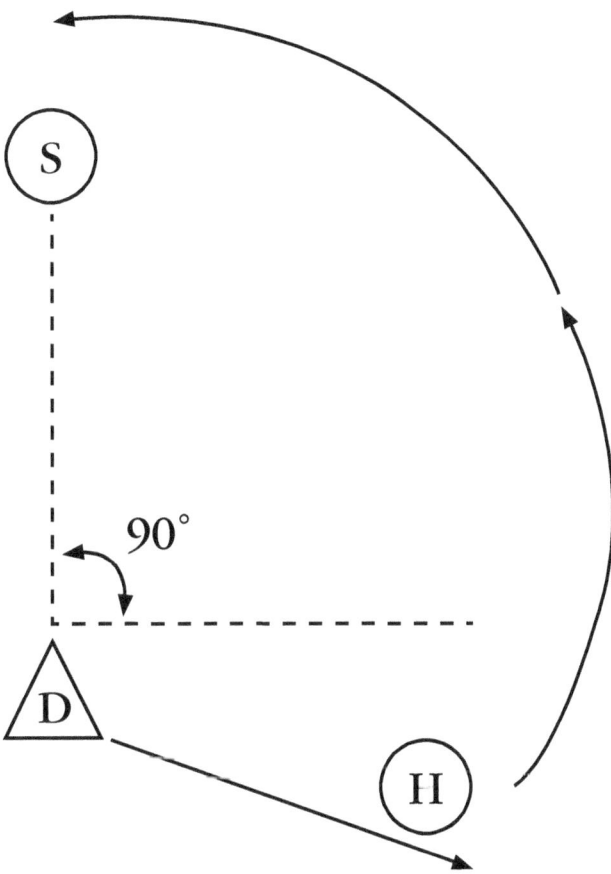

The handler's position is behind the dog and to the side of the desired flank. The dog moves at **more than** a 90° angle in order to come around the handler. By emphasizing turning away from the stock, this can be refined to produce a square flank.

the stock to bring them back. I like to start this early in the training at the stage when he is first fetching stock to me. If I always allow the dog to break and cover stock every time the sheep go past me, I find that he will want to do this when I start driving. If I teach him to push sheep off and past me early in his training, it is much easier to teach him to drive.

Clockface Exercise

Once I have the dog pushing sheep off and past me, I will begin flanking and stopping him off balance. If you visualize a clock and stop your dog at 2 o'clock, a walk up would take the sheep in a straight line to 8 o'clock. If you stop him at 11 o'clock, a walk up would take the sheep in a straight line to 5 o'clock. (Diagram 2). You may only move from 2 to 6 or 7 steps with the dog in order to push the sheep past you and on for a few feet. I will be walking off to one side of the dog. I will make sure that I have the dog move sheep past me by walking past me on both my right and left sides. I will try to stop the dog at a variety of positions on the clockface. You will need to flank the dog both directions around the face of the clock. This includes moving away from you and coming past you when you flank him back in the opposite direction. After you have done this as outside flanks you will also do the clockface exercise with inside flanks.

Inside Flanks

Most of what you have done with your dog during early training stages will be outside flanks. But, to complete your dog's education you will also have to do inside flanks. I like to start inside flanks as soon as the dog is fetching and I can flank him both directions and stop him.

Passing Across In Front of the Handler

I will usually start in a small enclosure (30-50' square or oval pen). I stand in the center and let the sheep drift out toward the fence. At first I will start with the dog on leash. I will have the dog walk up

Diagram 2
___

The Clock Face Exercise

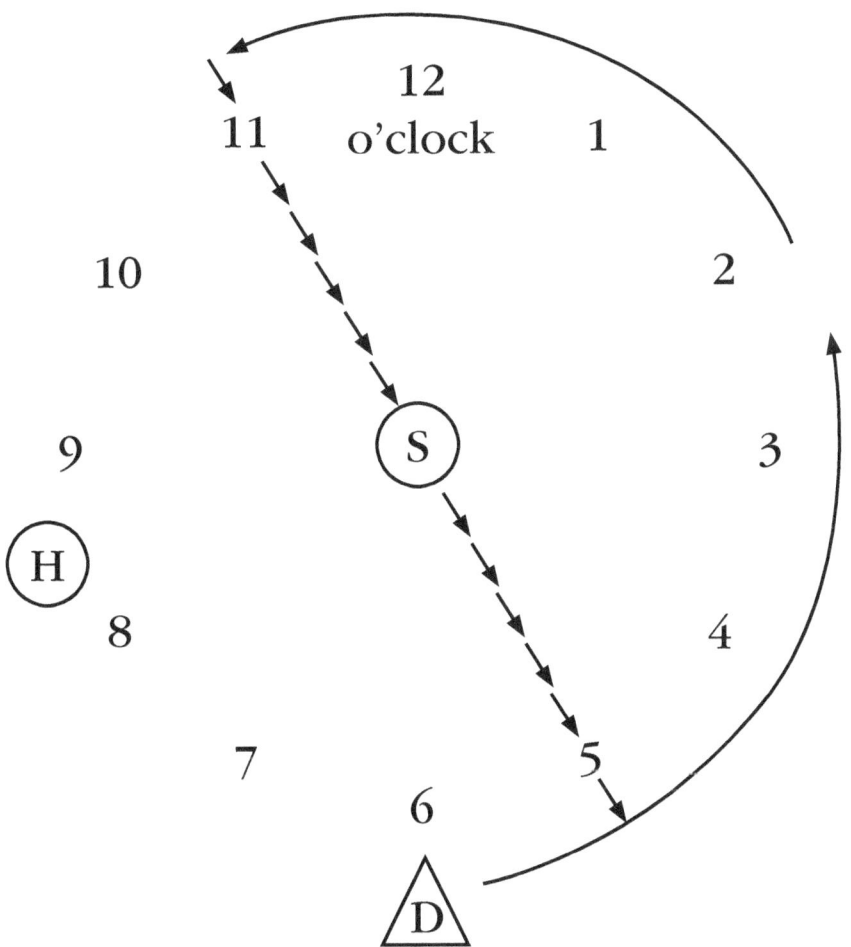

This exercise is to teach the dog to push sheep past you (beginning the drive) and should be done on both sides and from a variety of positions on the clock face. At first, the dog may only need to move the sheep 6 or 7 steps past you.

toward the sheep and have to dog a short distance in front of me. I will teach him to be comfortable passing in front of me by asking him to do very short flanks while helping him by guiding him by the leash. If I start with the dog slightly ahead of me and on my right side, I will stop him, transfer the leash from my right to my left hand across the front of my body. I will take a step back and pull the dog across in front of me. As he comes across in front of me, I will give him a COME BY command. I will let him flank a short distance past me and stop him again and have him walk up a few steps to the sheep until I see the sheep move only a small amount. Then I'll step back and repeat this in the other direction. The dog will be slightly in front of you and on your left side. Transfer the leash from your left hand to your right hand. Take a step backwards and pull the dog across in front of you, telling him AWAY TO ME as he comes across in front of you. Let him flank a short distance (several feet) past you and then stop him and walk him up a few steps until you see a small amount of movement of the sheep.

Sometimes you may have to take a step in the direction that you want the dog to move at the same time that you are taking a step backwards. This will help guide him in the direction you want him to go. If you need more room between you and the sheep, you can BACK him or call him off, reposition and start again. The purpose is to flank the dog, not to move the sheep.

When you can get the dog to do this, put a longer rope on him and position yourself farther from the dog. Ask him to take longer flanks while moving across in front of you. The distance that you ask him to walk up and move stock can also gradually increase. Since you are farther from the sheep than the dog, you will be covering a longer distance from side to side than the dog will be. This will necessitate a lot of walking. Don't forget to step back in order to make sure that the dog makes a rounded arc around the stock instead of flat flanks.

Driving Sheep Around a Pen

Once the dog will pass across in front of the handler, as described above, I will start asking him to drive sheep around a pen. I like to use sheep that are light enough to move away from the dog easily, but not so light that they will want to run away. If you do not use the right type of sheep for this exercise it can create problems and will be very difficult because the sheep with either be sticking like glue to the handler or running away. If you do not have the correct type of sheep or find that you are having problems with this exercise, you may have to undertake some of the exercises described for driving and then come back to this exercise.

I will do this exercise in the same small enclosure (30-50' square or oval pen). I stand in the center and let the sheep drift out toward the fence. I usually will let the dog drag the 15' rope. I will start the dog on a flank and when he gets to approximately 3 or 9 o'clock, I'll stop him and ask him to WALK UP, allowing him to push the sheep a short distance so that they pass between me and the fence. If the sheep come off the fence and closer to me, I will ask him to flank back toward me. If he is reluctant to flank, I'll also say 'here' to get him to come toward me. I'll stop him and tell him to WALK UP so that he can put the sheep back on line to drive in the direction in which he originally started. My object is to teach the dog to drive the sheep around the small pen, using flanks, as needed, to keep the sheep along the outside part of the pen and moving around it. While I am doing this I will try to be facing the direction that the sheep are moving around the pen, with my shoulders perpendicular to the sheep and the dog and my body between the dog's shoulder and hip. I may have to move in a small circle within the center of the pen or take a small step back in order to keep from getting in front of the dog's eye as he drives the sheep around the pen. This positioning is a very important part of this exercise.

While I'm doing this exercise I will also be working on stopping the dog for short instances and asking him to walk up. I will be using my flank commands to get him to come toward me or away from me. If he does not want to flank towards me or refuses a flank, I can take a step to the front of him and place my rake or other training aid between the dog and the sheep, but closer to the sheep. Then I will ask him to flank, accompanied by here to make him come my direction.

I will stop him before he comes all the way past me. If needed, I can move the rake out to the opposite side by moving it across my body or transferring it from one hand to the other in order to keep him from moving past me. This exercise will take practice. If you are consistent, you should be able to make steady progress and should be able to drive sheep around the pen smoothly.

Later you will combine inside flanks with more extended driving. This will be covered in more detail in the Chapter on The Drive.

With inside flanks, flattening or cutting in can be a problem. Make sure that the dog keeps his flanks square or rounded. Don't try to drive long distances or do long flanks. Keep the drive and the flanks short so that you do not get into trouble.

Short and Long and Fast and Slow Flanks

You will want to be able to tell your dog to flank fast or slow and to flank a short distance or long distance around the sheep. This will help you accurately position him and help him learn to do various tasks that require precision and accuracy. The distinction between precision and accuracy is important—being in the right place is being accurate; being able to hit the right place repeatedly is being precise! You will need both precision and accuracy when placing your dog relative to the sheep.

When you are using your flanking commands, you can use a short or abbreviated word or part of the regular flanking command (BY or COME instead of COME BY and WAY instead of AWAY TO ME) or a shortened whistle in order to get a short flank. At first you may have to be ready to give the command and stop your dog very quickly when he has only gone a short distance. By drawing out and lengthening the command verbally or with a whistle, you will be able to lengthen the flank and/or make it wider. This may require that you step in and give your dog an OUT or a BACK to show him that the flank should be longer and wider. For most handlers, I would recommend that you have 3 flanks—a short one, a regular one and a long/wide flank. There are an almost infinite number of variations that you can communicate by your tone and degree of urgency, the way you say the command, how rapidly you give the flank, and whether or not you repeat it.

The speed of the flank will be influenced by your tone, whether you have a rising inflection at the end of the command and by repetition of the command. If you use a rising inflection and rapidly repeat the command, this will speed the dog up. If you use a command or whistle whose parts are slower or separated by slight pauses or a command with a downward inflection or in combination with the word STEADY this may help the dog learn that you want him to take the command but to do it at a slower pace. This is particularly helpful when you are working in confined quarters or with sheep that may be easily started if the dog were to move more quickly.

If you will be aware that you want to have these types of variations in your commands when you are starting out, this will help you chose commands that can be modified in a way to communicate these distinctions to your dog.

You will need to practice short and long and fast and slow flanks close at hand and then at increasing distances. Concentrate on giving commands in the same way each time so that you are consistent. The more consistent you are, the faster your dog will learn. If you want a short flank, be prepared to enforce it, just as you would any other command—if your dog does not go only a short distance, stop him and make a correction. This is important in enforcing all the types of flanks that you will be using.

Concluding Remarks

Flanking is important in all aspects of work and trialing. If you don't have flanks, you do not have a way to steer your dog. Having power steering is the result of consistent work and practice.

THE STOP

Introduction

A stop is an essential part of herding. You need to be able to accurately stop your dog at almost any time. You will need to be able to make him lie down or stand and should have separate commands for these. I prefer to teach the dog to stop standing before teaching the lie down. This is because once they learn to lie down it seems to be harder to teach them to stop on their feet.

Teaching Stand and Down

You can teach both of these commands to your pup and young dog while he is on leash and away from the sheep. You can teach stand by walking with the dog. Say 'stand' or whatever command you have chosen for this command. If he lies down or sits, I'll go pick him up and put him on his feet.

If the dog is a big dog or it is difficult for you to pick him up or get him back on his feet, you can attach a rope to his collar and run the rope down his back and through another collar or loop the rope around his flank and tie it with a Bowlin Knot so that is does not tighten up around his flank (Diagram 3). You can then lift up on the rope or collar to keep him on his feet as you come to a stop and ask him to stand. If you need to pick him up, you can slide your foot underneath

Diagram 3

Bowlin Knot

A Bowlin knot is used so that pressure on the rope will not cause the rope to tighten up around the dog's flank.

his belly—this will help keep him on his feet since he will be uncomfortable trying to lie down on top of your foot.

When you can reliably get him to stand, you will want to be able to walk away from him and around him without him moving. If, when walking around him, the dog wants to turn around and follow you, just stop your progress and turn and walk the opposite way around the dog. This will keep him from turning around and following you. Gradually increase the distance you go around the dog until you can walk all the way around him and at various distances from him. He may turn his head to watch you, but shouldn't move his feet. I do not feel that a stay command should be given in order to get the dog to stay in position. Once you have told him to stand or lie down he should stay in that position until told to move.

At this point, it is very important that you do not put too much pressure on the dog if he lies down or moves. It usually just makes the problem worse and makes him uncomfortable on his feet. You want to make him comfortable on his feet. Later you may have to more forcefully correct the dog, but be sure to keep him comfortable during the early stages of teaching this command. Another thing to be aware of: after the dog has been taught to down and gains experience with stock, you may have him on a stand while holding stock. But, if the stock is quiet and the dog does not perceive a need to stay on his feet he may conserve his energy and lie down. He is not being disobedient, just being sensible! If there is movement of the sheep or he is needed to catch or hold he should be back on his feet and ready to respond.

To teach the 'lie down' you will again be walking with the dog. In order to help encourage him to lie down without forcing him to lie down, you can step on the rope up close to the attachment to the collar. This will pull his head down and eventually he will decide for himself that it is more comfortable for the rest of the body to follow and will lie down. This is usually easier than trying to force a dog to lie down by pushing on his body and struggling to tackle him until he and you are both flat on the ground.

If the dog wants to sit rather than lie down, you can gently massage the dog between the shoulders until he relaxes. Gently rock him back and forth and as he relaxes, you will be able to gently push him over on one side to get him to lie down without much force.

Some dogs when they are around stock and the stock is moving they will be so interested in the stock that they will forget the 'lie down' and 'stand' commands that you have taught them away from the stock. You will have to remind them of these commands and practice them in the vicinity of the stock. If this does not work, I take a 6' leash and snap it to his collar, run it down under the lowest bar of a fence or under a fence post and then tie him with his head approximately 3-4" from the ground. I prefer to be able to run the rope under something low and then tie it up higher. If he begins to fight or panic I then have easy access to untie him without having to reach down to where he is. While he is tied, I will walk a short distance away from him so that I can keep an eye on him and will be close enough to release him, if needed. I will let him pull against himself and he will eventually give in and lie down. Then it will take a period of time before he is comfortable lying down and will not worry about stock moving around and by him. Once he is beginning to accept this restraint, I may work stock with another dog relatively close to him so that he will experience some pressure that may make him want to break out of this position. You do not want to create panic or unnecessary fight within the dog, but need to be sure that he will stay lying down and become comfortable lying down with stock working increasingly close to him. Eventually you may be able to tie him to the side of a pen and work sheep within the pen or an adjacent enclosure without him becoming upset or fighting being tied. Once the dog will do this, I may have the dog by my side while watching other people work dogs. This way he learns to honor other dogs and people working and will be comfortable lying down and waiting for his turn to work stock without becoming too excited. This is very handy at trials and in working situations when multiple dogs are present.

The 'lie down' is also useful in any situation in which multiple dogs and strange dogs may be present since you can control your dog and put him in a submissive position (lying down) that may prevent fighting or confrontation with other dogs that would be more likely to occur if he was on his feet.

Practice having your dog lie down and let other dogs move by or come up and smell him. Do not let him get up. This will help him become comfortable or at least learn to tolerate other dogs so that there is less likelihood of a fight or confrontation developing. I also like this because it keeps my dog out of other people's space and their dog's space—it is important to me that my dog does not invade others' space. It is impolite for him to intrude upon another person's or dog's space or territory. This is one reason that I do not encourage my dog to go to other people and let other people pet him. If people want to pet my dog I will have my dog lie down and then have them go to the dog to pet him, rather than allowing the dog to go to the person. This helps ensure that he will be obedient in crowds or social situations and not become a pest, nuisance or a threat.

If you don't like people in your face, think about how it would feel to have a dog run up to you or another dog and crowd into his space! At the very least it is uncomfortable and, at the worst, it could be dangerous.

Stand and Lie Down While On Stock

You will have to practice many stops while on stock to get the dog consistent in stopping how and when you want him to. I like to flank my dog around the sheep, stop him, let him stand for a few seconds, then flank again, stop, have him BACK, then walk up, then flank again. Be careful to not have the dog BACK too often after stopping since this may cause him to release pressure on the stock every time he stops.

I try to stop the dog in a variety of places relative to the stock and in a variety of situations so that he becomes comfortable stopping, regardless of how fast he may be traveling or what distance he is from me. I will let the dog bring the sheep to me and then stop him. I will then try to push the sheep toward him to see if he will give to the pressure, hold or dive in. I would prefer that he holds his position and wait to see what happens. If the sheep break and try to get around him he will need to cover them and bring them back and then stand again. I may walk out to him and briefly touch him on the head or body, then walk back to the stock. I may catch a sheep, examine its mouth or feet and make sure that he will hold his standing position without moving.

When you have stopped a dog so that he is holding sheep, he should have the ability to move appropriately in order to hold the sheep. This means that he will sometimes have to break from his standing position in order to control and hold the stock; he should not have to stop and stay stopped without regard for the stock and what is happening. But, you do not want him to move when there is no reason to do so. Some young dogs will become bored or will not be comfortable staying stopped. They will want to create movement, excitement and entertainment for themselves. You do not want to leave the dog too long at a stand or lie down, especially during the early stages of training. The length of time that you will expect him to stay stopped will increase as he understands and matures.

With the lie down, you will NOT want the dog to move to cover the stock, as we wanted when he was standing and holding stock. You will want to push the stock toward the dog and have him remain lying down. If you allow the dog to break the lie down in order to cover the stock, you will find that your 'lie down' rapidly disappears! Once the dog is lying down he should only move when you have asked him to get up. If you allow him to move without asking him to do so, you will find that he may decide to move whenever he wants. This can create big problems for you and often it will become difficult or impossible to get him to lie down and stay down when you need him to.

Another problem that you will see is the dog that will lie down in the front, but keeps his hind end in the air! The dog is anticipating the command to move. Make him lie all the way down and wait. It may be helpful to walk up to him and push or pull him over onto one hip so that he lies down. Vary the time you make him wait before giving him another command. Even if the sheep are escaping he should learn to lie down and be patient and wait for you to tell him to move. A variation on this is the dog that has his toenails dug into the ground and wants to pull himself forward on his belly as he is lying on the ground. Make this dog lie down and keep him down until he will relax and wait. The exercise of tying the dog low on the fence and working sheep nearby will often help this type of dog learn to accept the pressure of nearby sheep.

In order to help dogs that do these things, I prefer to have the dog learn to lie down and put his chin on the ground between his front legs. I start this when I stand on the rope when teaching them to lie down. You may have to push his head down physically. Chances are his head will pop right back up and you will have to push it down repeatedly. You may feel like you are dribbling a basketball after a while! But, the dog will eventually learn to lie down and keep his head down no matter what! He will learn to stay down until asked to move again.

Enforcing the Lie Down at a Distance

You will find that with increasing distance from you, your dog may not accurately take the 'lie down' command. You will have to move out there and enforce this command. It does not matter if you have to walk or run or ride a long distance to do this. Your dog should know that you will enforce the command, regardless of how far away he is. You cannot expect the dog to have the lie down happen if you are too lazy to go out to your dog and enforce it. Once you have made that walk out toward him, you will find that you may not have to walk very far toward him in order to enforce the lie down the next time. Once you have moved toward the dog and enforced the command you do not need to continue to go all the way out to him. You will only have to go all the way out to him if he will not respond to a lesser correction.

THE BACK AND OUT

Introduction

The BACK and OUT commands are very useful, but you will find that few handlers may think about putting these commands on their dogs. BACK tells the dog to move directly away from the stock without turning his face away from them. OUT tells the dog to move further away from the stock while flanking. I usually start teaching the BACK first; it is easier to teach this before teaching the OUT because it is a more strenuous execution for the dog. Once you have taught the OUT the dog may want to move as he would for the OUT command, instead of moving straight back for the BACK.

Teaching the BACK

If I have a puppy or a young dog up to 18 months of age that I am starting, I will start teaching the BACK as soon as they are leading nicely on leash. I have a gate that I walk through with my dogs several times each day. When I come to the gate, I stop the puppy so that when I pull the gate open it comes towards him and he will step back. As he steps back, I'll tell him to BACK. If you do not have a gate, use a doorway. Use the leash to keep him from turning his head or turning around. At first he may only take 1 step back. It is usually easier to get him to move his front feet than his back feet. Gradually you may increase the distance that you expect him to move back.

Once the dog figures out that he can move his back feet, the back begins to come easier. Now that he understands that he can move his back feet, I'll move to the next step.

At this stage I will position my dog along a fence with me in front of him. I use a plastic rake as a training tool. I will tap the rake lightly in front of his front leg that is farthest forward and tell him to BACK. He will usually pull that foot back and I'll then tap at the other front foot to encourage him to move back. If you try to make him back up too quickly, the front feet will overrun the back feet and the dog will sit down. If he does sit down, you might have to put a suitcase handle on him to pick up the back or front end to help him to learn to back (see Chapter on The Stop).

Some dogs may take a long time to learn this. Do it three or four times a day. The longest that I've spent is a year—it took that long before the dog became comfortable backing up. Now it backs fine and will back up anywhere, whenever I ask.

For older dogs, you can use a hallway or make a 8' long chute along a fence. The chute should be narrow enough that he cannot turn sideways or turn around. You may have to have a leash on him to keep his head facing you.

Once I get the dog to back away from me, I'll walk along the outside of the chute and put my training aid in front of the dog and ask him to back out of it. When he can back the full length of it, I will walk him up to the mouth of the chute and ask him to back without him being in the chute. Don't be in a hurry to do this out in the open; it may take a while to get the dog comfortable using his back legs and to build up the muscles he uses when backing.

Some dogs will move back if you step out in front of them and shake the leash up and down. When the dog understands the word BACK, then drop the leash and make sure he will BACK when you are in various positions relative to the dog. I ask my dog to BACK in a lot of situations so it becomes very natural to them. I only want the dog to BACK when I ask him to. He may step back in order to cover stock that is breaking, but shouldn't step back when I am asking him to hold pressure on the stock.

Remember to only have the dog BACK up a few steps during the early training—if you make him continue to back up until he is uncomfortable he will not want to BACK the next time. Just like teaching the lie down, gradually lengthen the BACK over time and as the dog understands the command.

Teaching the OUT

I don't seriously train a puppy to OUT, but I will lay the foundation for this by teaching the puppy to be a good citizen and this includes getting out of things and moving away from me (as go over there and lie down). I usually will want a young dog to be working well before I start teaching the OUT. Be aware that, not only should your pup or young dog learn to come TO you, he should also learn to move AWAY from you. Make him move if you want to move past him in the house—don't go around him or step over him. Another good thing to make all dogs do, is learn to WAIT until you are ready for them to do something. This is a handy command to have for everyday living. Make him wait until you tell him to move before going in and out of doors or in and out of the car or kennel. You may teach them this by using a word for it (such as WAIT).

When a dog is moving well around his stock and will go both directions and do short fetches to me, I will start teaching the OUT. Dogs that you have raised from pups or dogs that you have worked with will already know to move away from you with pressure. It will be easier to teach them to move out and away from the sheep. It may take more persistence and intimidation with a dog that has not had this foundation training.

In order to teach the OUT, I will walk up to the sheep on leash. I'll tell the dog OUT and then turn around and take him out and away from sheep for a short distance. When he gets to the point that HE will make the initial move to move out, then I'll put the sheep in a corner. I'll be on the far side of the sheep with the sheep between me and the dog. I'll stop him on the far side of the sheep and ask him to OUT. If he does not do it, then I'll go through the sheep and go right to him in order to enforce the OUT. This teaches him that he must move OUT, regardless of what position I am in relative to him or the sheep.

Once he has mastered this, then I will step out to one side or the other of the sheep in the corner. I'll ask the dog to walk up so that he and I are roughly parallel and the same distance from the sheep. Then I'll stop him and ask him to OUT. If he does not do it, then I can step in front of him and enforce the OUT.

Once he is competent at doing this, I will place the sheep out in the open and flank the dog around the sheep. If he starts to come in (and all of them WILL, at some point in time!), then I will stop him and tell him to OUT. If he does not move out, then I will step in front of him and enforce the out and lie him down again. I will stop him before he stops himself—it is important to make him stop where and when YOU want him to, not when he wants to. I want to stop him before he stops himself. I will then walk back to where I was when I originally gave the command. I will give him a flank in the same direction as before and stop him when he gets to the opposite side of the sheep. The reason I walk back to where I was originally is to make sure that the dog has learned to stay off and is taking responsibility for doing this, not just because I was between him and the sheep, holding him off the sheep. By doing this you will determine if the dog has truly learned the meaning of OUT. It is a little extra walking, but is well worth the effort!

After the dog will take the OUT from a stop, then I will ask him to take the OUT while moving. I would like to see him bubble out, making a definite curve out in his path as he goes around the sheep. If he does not IMMEDIATELY move out and away from the sheep, making a bubble in his path, I will stop him and walk toward him, enforcing the OUT command. If you do not enforce this command, pretty soon you will be repeatedly saying OUT, but there may not be any change in his path around the sheep. Make sure the OUT does not turn into a flank command. You should see a definite widening of the flank on the OUT command. If you do not see a change in it, go back and work on the basics until this is correctly executed.

If you have let your dog continually disobey the OUT command, you may have to go back and put another word to this command and retrain this command since the dog has learned to ignore the OUT command. It will be just like the lie down. If you will take the time to go out to the dog and make the correction during the learning stages of training, later you will find that you may only have to go a short ways toward the dog in order to enforce this command. He should OUT on both outside flanks (when you are between him and sheep) and inside flanks (when the dog is between you and the sheep).

An equally important part is calling of teaching maneuverability while flanking and on the outrun, is having the ability to also call you dog IN on his flanks or outrun. Once dogs have learned to move OUT and learn to bend out on an outrun, they may go too wide. This is where you will want to teach him to come in and stay in contact with his sheep. This may happen if the dog is running without thinking about where his sheep are, if he has been pushed out too far or if the terrain or circumstances may lead him to run wider than desired. If you see that he is running too wide, then ask him to "here, here" to draw him in to the sheep. If this does not work, you may have to stop him, walk him up toward the sheep until he is back in contact and then flank him again. This way you have both ends of the OUT. You are able to get him to move toward or away from his sheep while on the move.

Concluding Remarks

The BACK and OUT, as with most things you will be doing with your dog, are not perfected overnight. It takes a long period of time to refine these commands so that you can place your dog accurately and with a high degree of precision. You cannot hurry these commands and expect the dog to keep a good attitude and continue to perform at a high standard.

THE WALK UP

Introduction

The WALK UP is an essential part of working stock. Many dogs will advance on stock on their own because they want to create movement. But, the true test comes when you ask the dog to WALK UP in a variety of situations. It requires a confident dog to walk up to stock in a controlled manner, exerting steady and even pressure without excessive force to move his stock. It is when you have stock that don't easily move away from the dog that you will see whether or not he will truly WALK UP to move stock and HOW he walks up to exert quiet power and authority to move his stock. Some dogs may sneak up on their stock, pulling the stock to them and making them difficult to move, while the dog with natural ability and good training will walk up with quiet authority and a confident attitude that will result in the desired movement of the stock. Other dogs may communicate panic and uncertainty to their stock and cause the stock to move off with panic or confusion. Usually the posture of this dog will be evident—his head will be in toward the sheep and his inside shoulder will be dropped down toward the stock. This may be evident during the latter point of the outrun, usually starting at the point where the dog passes the sheep on his arc. The dog with confidence may have his head turned in toward the stock, but his inside shoulder will be up (not dropped toward the stock). This part of the outrun and flanks affect the lift and the way that the dog will walk up and move his stock (See the Chapter on The Outrun) for additional information regarding the outrun and its relationship to the lift and walk up.

Teaching the WALK UP

The WALK UP starts, like many commands, when you have your puppy or young dog where they will walk on a leash. When you take him around the stock on leash, turn toward the sheep and walk towards the sheep and let him stand and watch them as they move away. You are doing a WALK UP. If you have the opportunity to feed the sheep, you can walk him up to push the sheep off of the feed trough. You can let him stand and hold them (on leash) while you put out the feed. If the sheep break, just push them away again. But, if you do not have daily access to sheep, you may want to spend some time teaching the dog to walk up to the sheep. I prefer to walk into their faces. As they move away, have the dog stop and stand and watch them move off. Then turn and call the dog off (THAT'LL DO) and pat him. You may repeat this several times, but don't need a large number of repetitions on a single day. As the dog gets better at walking up you should begin to note his reactions. Some dogs will want to run right up into the sheep. Other dogs will only walk up so close to the sheep and then will not continue to advance. They may lie down or turn their head away to avoid the pressure from the sheep. Both of these types of dogs are uncomfortable with themselves and the situation. Other dogs are willing to walk right up and stand there and allow the sheep to move off; this dog is comfortable with himself and the situation.

The dogs that wanted to dive in or to avoid walking up have identical problems. Both are reacting to pressure. When a dog dives in, he does this to alleviate the pressure by diving in and getting the sheep to move off. The second dog wants to avoid the pressure and holds back. You will have to get both of these dogs comfortable with themselves while under pressure.

For the dog that dives in, walk him up just to the point where he wants to dive in. Stop him and let him stand until he relaxes. If he goes to dive in and bite, you will have to be ready to make a correction and keep him from making contact with the sheep. You may have to make a strong physical correction to keep him from damaging the sheep. A muzzle may be required if you are not willing or capable of making this type of correction quickly and accurately.

For the dog that wants to avoid pressure and will not walk up, you will need to walk up until he will not continue to do so. Then pat and reassure him and try to encourage him to walk up with you. Do not drag or force the dog to walk toward the stock or he will become even more reluctant to approach them. If he is still very reluctant and he will not walk up, I try to change the situation so that they will learn to be comfortable with sheep close around them.

To work with both these types of dogs, I use what I call the packed sheep pen exercise.

The Packed Sheep Pen Exercise

I take 5-10 sheep and put them in a 10 x 10 to 12 x 12 enclosure or any small area within which the sheep will be fairly closely packed together. I call this the packed sheep pen exercise. I will forget about anything else I've been doing with the dog up to this point and concentrate on getting him over this in order to advance in my training. Enter the packed pen with the dog on leash. Start walking around the outside of the pen.

Encourage him to make a hole and push through in order to walk around the periphery of the pen. With the aggressive dog that wants to dive in an bite, you may have to hold him with or very close to the collar since your encouragement may result in him jumping forward and wanting to bite the sheep. If he jumps out to bite, you may have to give him a slap on the nose just as he wants to jump forward and bite. Continue to crowd your way around the outside of the pen. Do this in both directions. If one of the sheep wants to butt or push back at the dog, then he is allowed to jump forward and take a bite. Continue to do this until the dog will flank around the outside on his own with little or no restraint on the leash. Then you can move to the outside of the pen and flank him around both directions while he is inside the pen. I have quite good luck in using this exercise with young dogs.

If dogs have established bad habits it may take more time to break these and have the dog become comfortable and trustworthy in this situation. Some dogs have been taught or allowed to bite when a certain level of pressure has built up, particularly out in the open; I call this a 'trigger response.' If this is not corrected early in their training it may be very difficult to remedy or retrain. This exercise may help this type of dog to some degree, but these dogs may never be trustworthy in high pressure circumstances. So, if you see this response in your young dog or pup, you better get him in and get him over it very quickly! This exercise is the best way I have found to do that.

For the dog that is reluctant to walk up on the sheep and does not want to dive in and bite, you will have to help him in order to get him to walk around the periphery of the pen. You may need to push a sheep out of the way or help make a hole for him to walk into. In the initial stages, if a sheep wants to butt the dog, you may have slap the sheep on the nose or help turn it so that it does not hit the dog. This way the dog will learn that you are there to help him and, as he becomes more comfortable, he will begin to help you and move sheep himself. You will praise and encourage him when he does so. Gradually he will start moving around the stock. Usually he will then concentrate on going around, but may not be concentrating on the sheep. One of the sheep may butt him as he goes around. Encourage the dog to come back and get a hold of this sheep. You will have to push the sheep's head down at the dog and encourage him to grip. Even if he does not grip, but just makes a move toward the sheep, release the sheep so that it moves away. He will think that he has done this. Encourage and praise him for this move. It will show him that you are there and working together. Sometimes you will have to place yourself so that the dog is between you and the sheep and make it more comfortable for the dog to go into the sheep than to come toward you. There is no magic way to do this.....you will have to create more pressure on the dog than the sheep are. You will not have to resort to this often, but occasionally there will be a dog that needs this type of situation.

This exercise should only be conducted for short sessions. You may do this several times a day for 5 or 10 minutes, at most.

This exercise also should be used for the dog with confidence that walks up naturally. It is an important part of his education to learn to be in very close contact with sheep and to learn to accept this pressure. It will likely be easier to do this exercise with this type of dog than the previous two types. But, don't neglect the steps—start out on leash and progress through the stages until you can flank him around inside the pen in either direction while you are standing outside the pen.

I would do this for several sessions until the dog is quite comfortable. I would do this at the beginning of the training session and then go work on something else.

After I have the dog working well in the packed pen, I will set up a V-shaped pen by placing a panel across the corner of an enclosure. I would like it to be at least 10-16' from the point of the V to the enclosing panel (Diagram 4). I will put 4-5 sheep in this. I will put the dog on the long side of the enclosure and some distance from this v-shaped pen. I will stand at the center of the enclosing panel so that I can see the dog walking down the fence toward the pen. I will walk him toward the sheep. He will be walking down the side of the enclosure toward the sheep. This is a good place to work on having him stop and BACK periodically as he approaches the sheep in the pen. I will walk him up 2-3 times. Then I will ask the dog to go into the V-shaped pen and bring them out of the pen. If the sheep get too packed into the narrow portion of the V, you may have to pull the enclosing panel further out in order to give the dog enough room to get around the sheep and bring them out. You may have to go with the dog on a leash to help him move the sheep out of this type of pen. A common reaction is for the dog to want to grab the sheep as they move past him as him takes them out of the V. Help him learn not to do this by restraining him and allowing the sheep to leave and move past him. As he gains expertise in this shape pen you may be

Diagram 4

Use of the V-Shaped Pen

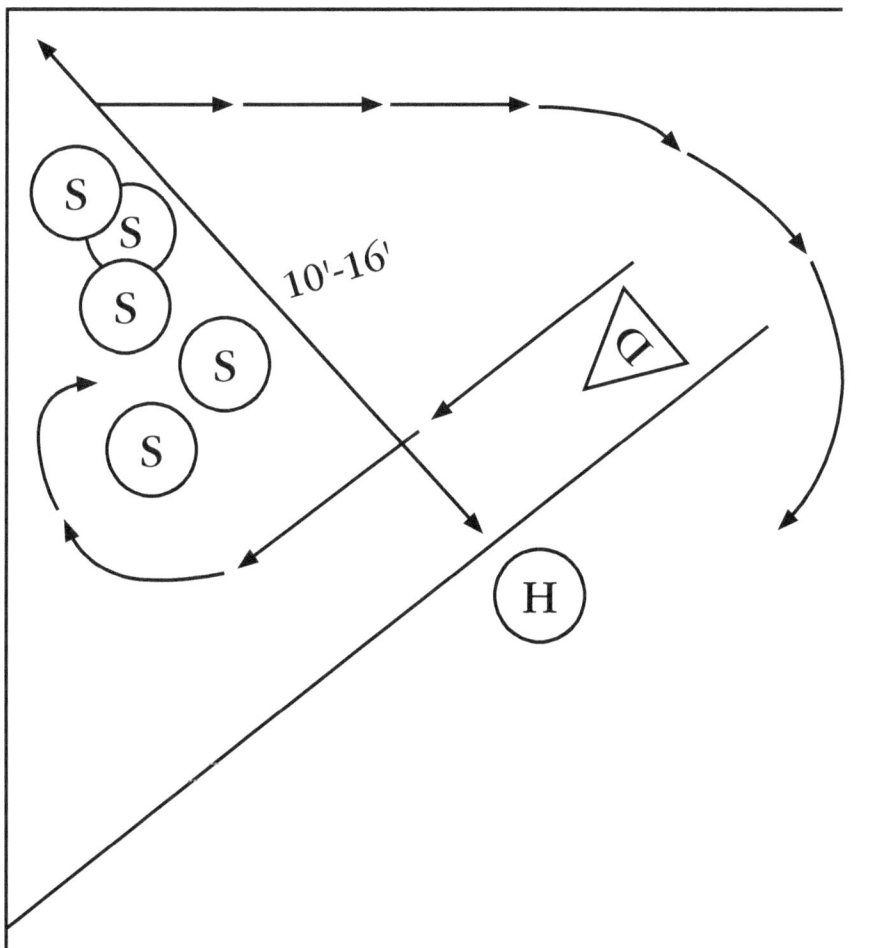

The handler asks the dog to move along the long side of the V-shaped pen in order to go around the sheep and move them out of the pen.

able to close it back up. When all the sheep have moved out of the pen, stop your dog, call him to you and pet him. Send him around and put the sheep back into the pen and repeat it. Two to three times is sufficient for this exercise and it should improve with work over several sessions.

Walk Up to a Tied Sheep

Another exercise that is helpful for teaching the Walk Up is walking up on a tied sheep. The purpose of this exercise is to teach the dog to handle pressure, to WALK UP and to BACK out of pressure when you ask him to. It is not to have the dog bite the sheep for no reason.

I like to start with the dog approximately 30' down the fence from the sheep's head. I stand with the dog between me and the fence, with my leg at his shoulder. I will encourage him to look at the sheep. If he will not look at the sheep at this time, don't worry about it. I will ask the dog to walk up, being careful to observe his reactions as we approach the sheep. As you both walk toward the sheep, you will find that some dogs will look away and avoid looking at the sheep, other dogs will want to lie down or not move forward toward the sheep, and some dogs will want to dive in toward the sheep. The moment you see any of these things happening, you should stop. Let the dog stand there and relax. You can't make him look at the sheep if he does not want to. But, if he wants to lie down, I will lift him up and make him stand (use the suitcase handle if you need to). For the dog that wants to dive in, I'll hold the dog very close to or by the collar in order to restrain him. I like to have the dog stand on his feet and relax. Then I will ask the dog to BACK out of the pressure zone. I will get him comfortable at a distance and then repeat walking up toward the sheep. I will do this 3-4 times in a row. Then, when you have backed him off of the pressure, turn and walk away. Do not turn away when you have him close and feeling the pressure. Some days you will only gain inches; some days you will gain a foot. It usually will take 1-2 weeks to get the dog comfortable enough to walk all the way up to the sheep with you by his side. The sheep is liable to butt at your dog when he is up close. It is allowable for him to take a nip (quick bite and let go), but not a grip. After doing this, make sure he does not continue to go forward or advance on the sheep. This is why it is important to have a grip very close to his collar. Then back him out of the pressure and turn and walk away.

When the dog will walk up to the sheep with you by his side, I will step approximately 3-4' away from the dog, but still holding onto the leash and walk parallel to the dog as he walks up and backs doing this same exercise. If he will not take the BACK, I'll step slightly in front of his eye, stop him and back him up. I'll practice this until I am able to have him walk up to the sheep and back off calmly, as he did when I was directly by his side.

When he will do this, I will do the same things at 10-12' away, but still parallel to my dog. I will want to be able to get the same results as I did by his side and at 3-4' away. Be sure to step in and enforce the situation if he will not stop or back. When you can do this, try positioning yourself at different locations relative to the dog.

If, at any time, the dog starts diving in or hesitating, stop, go back to the previous step and keep bad habits from developing. Going back is not failing, it is just practicing the basics. Basics are the key to long-term success.

Continued Refinement of the Walk Up

You will be practicing the walk up frequently when working the sheep and doing other things. If you have the opportunity to walk your dog up, don't be afraid to walk him up. If he needs help to walk up confidently, don't be afraid to help and walk with him. But, don't get in the habit of helping the job before he tries. If he is not trying, you may need to put a little pressure on him to make him go forward—you can do this by blocking him with your body if he wants to leave the pressure. There is a fine balance in determining how hard to push in order to get the dog to go forward versus making him scared of you being behind him.

You will need to work on having your dog have several speeds on the walk up—he should go rapidly with encouragement to push the stock strongly, or steady and walk slowly to move the stock at a slower pace. When the dog is pushing stock forward you will have to allow him to go at the speed that will allow him to move the stock away, but, when he has light stock that will move away, you can work on having him move rapidly by encouraging him with your voice or asking him to walk slowly and steadily. Sometimes you may have to use a lie down or out if he is pushing too hard and will not steady as you would like. It isn't so much the speed of the dog, but the degree of pressure that the dog puts on the stock that causes them to move at speed. By using the OUT or BACK, you will get the dog to release the pressure and walk up with less pressure on his stock. By raising and speeding your voice up, you can communicate that you want more pressure and speed. I like to see if I can get the sheep going at a moderately fast pace. I will then make sure I can flank him while the stock is moving rapidly. This is instrumental in learning how to work a dog at speed. If you don't practice speeding the dog up, you will never be able to have the range of speeds that you need to reach a high standard. If you are working on one aspect—either fast or slow, make sure that you do not switch back and forth during the learning stages—if he doesn't speed up, don't then ask him to walk slow and vice versa. Make sure that you get the speed you want when you ask for it.

When you are asking the dog to push and increase the speed, make sure that he is behind the stock and not out to the side holding their eye and pulling them back to him. You may have to repeatedly flank him back behind the eye in order to keep him in the correct position and help him learn the position and purpose of what you are asking him to do.

Concluding Remarks

The walk up is an important part of you and your dog's ability to work stock. Being able to rely upon your dog to walk up when asked is a great thing. Do not take this aspect for granted—it requires as much practice as other commands that may have traditionally received more emphasis. Practice it fast and slow.

THE LOOK BACK

Introduction

The LOOK BACK command tells the dog to look farther away from sheep and is usually coupled with a flank command to tell the dog which direction to go. It is used if there may be sheep that the dog has missed on his original gather, sheep that he cannot see or sheep that are located in the distance. If the dog is trying to come in because he is confused about or doesn't know where the sheep are or is trying to cross the course, the LOOK BACK may be used to redirect him to find the sheep. It is also used as part of the double gather that is part of some types of trials—whereby the dog is sent for one group of sheep and takes them to a particular location and then is sent for a second group of sheep at another location. It is used following the shed or single when the dog needs to regroup the sheep prior to penning or exhausting the sheep.

You have to be careful that you do not use the LOOK BACK to make up for deficiencies in the dog's training that may cause him to leave a sheep or not keep a group of sheep together as he should on the fetch. I think the proper place to use the LOOK BACK is when the sheep are at a distance, not within a few feet of the dog. If you are interested in trialing, it is beneficial to teach this in a way that will be suitable for the double gather. If used for general work, it may not be necessary to have the same structure to the LOOK BACK, but this way to teach the LOOK BACK is suitable for any situation in which this command can be used.

Teaching the LOOK BACK

The LOOK BACK is best taught after the dog knows the basics of the outrun, lift and fetch. For the experienced handler, it is possible to take advantage of opportunities that happen during training or work when there are sheep in an appropriate location to teach the LOOK BACK. For those that do not have experience, you can use tied sheep in order to create a controlled situation or use a group of sheep that will stay in place and not try to rejoin a second group. Or, if you have a friend to help, have your friend hold a group of sheep at a distance. The tied sheep or group of sheep that will stay in one place or are being held have to be a sufficient distance away and you must have sufficient control of your dog to prevent the dog trying to go around the tied sheep without the LOOK BACK command. You should not have to use tied sheep for long; once your dog understands this exercise you should be able to use 2 groups of sheep free in the field. Be sure that you work this exercise in a both directions. You will want to make sure that you are not always tying or holding the sheep in the same place.

Then take another group of sheep and fetch them towards you. In order to establish a pattern or sequence of events that will eventually flow together as one continuous movement, you will want to make sure that you do the same things consistently and consistently get the desired response. To set up the pattern for the LOOK BACK, have the sheep at your feet and then flank the dog to either side—you will want to stop him between 1 and 2 o'clock or between 11 and 10 o'clock if you envision the clockface. Stop the dog and walk to the same side of the sheep as the dog and to your dog. Take him by the collar or a short rope and turn him around as you say LOOK BACK. You will want to turn him so that his head is turning away from the center of the clock (away from the sheep). For instance, if you have flanked him COME BY and stopped him about 2 o'clock, you will want him to turn back over his left shoulder so that he rotates away from the center of the clock and turns his head away from the sheep (Diagram 5). Stop him and make sure that he focuses on the group of sheep to be collected. If he does not focus on them immediately, you may have to walk with him toward the tied/held sheep until he sees them. Then send the dog around these sheep with a flank command. If he wants to go straight at the sheep or does not flank correctly, you may have to stop him and step between him and the sheep to enforce the command. If the dog does a nice flank, stop him on the opposite side of the sheep, release the tied sheep and let him fetch them to you in order to reward the dog's correct work.

    You do not have to release the sheep each time you do this. If tied with a long length of cord and properly acclimatized, you can let the dog walk toward them and move them only a short distance and then call him off. Then repeat the exercise. Or, you can flank the dog on around the sheep and call him off without moving the sheep. Once you are able to do this with two groups of sheep, you may want to use this exercise to help reinforce the shed by having the dog bring the second group of sheep a short ways to you and then flank him around and call him in between the groups as you would for a shed. Because the sheep are moving this will help make him come in fast and will keep you from having to separate the sheep repeatedly before setting up this exercise again. Once you've had him come in between the groups several times, make sure that you have the control to then flank him around the entire group of sheep so that he gathers both groups of sheep.

    When the dog turns off the first group of sheep, I prefer to have the dog learn to turn in a particular way in order to set up the direction for gathering the second group of sheep. For instance, if you will want to send him on a COME BY to pick up the second group of sheep, I would like him to turn over his left shoulder with a smooth transition to the flanking command. If he turns over his right should he will have to spin farther around in order to be positioned to take this command with a good, square flank. Just before giving the LOOK BACK command, you will give him a short flank in the direction opposite

Diagram 5

Teaching the Look Back

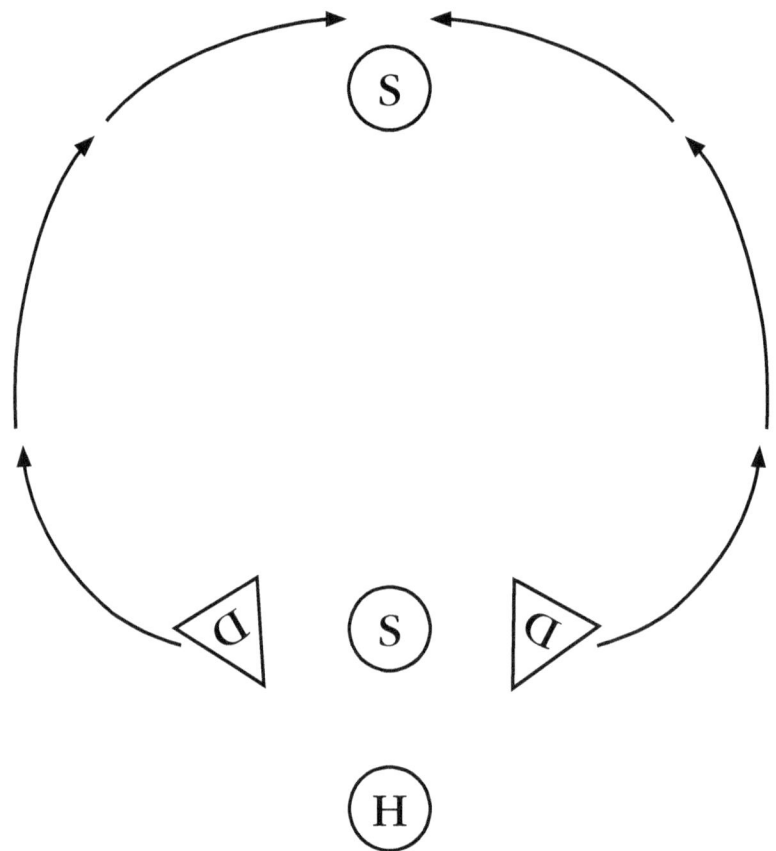

The point of the triangle is the dog's head. The dog on the left side of the diagram is positioned to do a look back with a come by flank. The arrow shows the direction his head should turn (over his right shoulder) to do the turn back. The dog on the right side of the diagram is positioned to do the look back with an away flank and should turn over his left shoulder (arrow).

to the direction of the flank that will accompany the LOOK BACK command (Diagram 6). For instance, if you want him to take a COME BY flank after the LOOK BACK, you will flank him a short ways to the AWAY TO ME (preparatory flank) side before asking him to LOOK BACK. The distance of the preparatory flank will help determine how wide he will run on the flank following the LOOK BACK. If the flank is short, the flank following the LOOK BACK will be shallower and usually shorter than if the distance of the preparatory flank is longer.

In order to help the dog learn to turn over the correct shoulder you will have to position yourself and walk toward him in a way that will help him turn in the correct direction. Most dogs will find turning one way easier than the other. You may have to have your dog LOOK BACK and then stop him, while you position yourself between him and the second group of sheep in order to get him to focus on and take the flank command for the second group of sheep. Eventually you will be able to ask him to LOOK BACK and give the flank command so that it is one continuous, flowing movement.

It is beneficial to not have the second group of sheep set up directly in line with the first group of sheep. Have the second group of sheep set off slightly to one side or the other. If you are going to send your dog on a COME BY flank for the second group of sheep, this group should be set off to the left of the handler as you are facing the dog across the first group of sheep. This will help ensure that the dog takes the COME BY flank and goes sufficiently deep and wide on his flank to get around the second group of sheep without startling or moving them from their position.

When your dog begins to understand this exercise, you begin to lengthen the distance he will have to go to pick up the second group of sheep and the distance that you are from the dog. You can also set the second group of sheep farther off to the side or out of sight as you refine this exercise. The dog should learn to trust you and that there are sheep out there to be gathered, even if he cannot see them when you ask him to LOOK BACK. This is a variation of sending your dog for sheep that he cannot see on his outrun.

Diagram 6

The Preparatory Flank for the Look Back

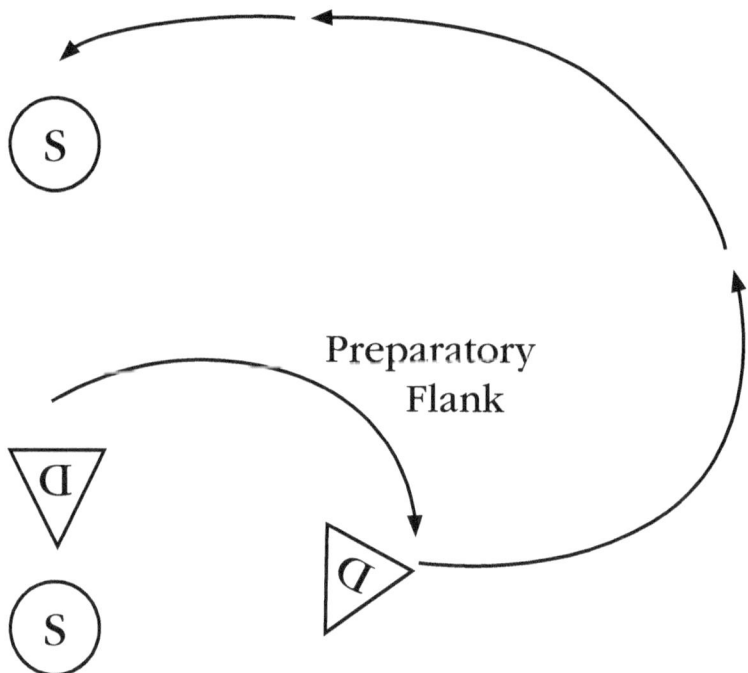

For a look back with an away flank, the dog is moved on a shorter preparatory come by flank, stopped, and then turned back and directed to the sheep with an away flank. The sequence is reversed when done on the other side.

The final goal is for you to be at a distance from the dog and the sheep, with the first group of the sheep between you and the dog when you give him the preparatory flank, the LOOK BACK and the finishing flank to gather the second group of sheep and bring them to join the first group. At the highest levels of competition, some dogs may have to run hundreds of yards to find sheep that are out of sight while doing a double gather.

Concluding Remarks

Mastering the LOOK BACK will take a considerable amount of time and practice. It will require that you help your dog in order to get him to execute the sequence of events in the order described above. Because it has multiple parts that may develop faults during execution, you may have to reinforce these parts periodically to make sure that the basics are sound and persistent.

Bob penning with Lynn

INFLUENCING THE EYE OF THE SHEEP

Introduction

This concept relates to the positioning of the dog or the handler relative to the sheep in order to influence movement of the sheep. It also relates to the position of the handler relative to the dog, especially during early training sessions when body language will be very important in communicating the direction and manner with which the dog will move around the stock.

In order to understand how to influence the eye of the sheep, picture yourself working with the sheep in a small enclosure without the dog or movements of the dog that will influence the sheep.

The handler or dog must catch the eye of the sheep in order to get the sheep to move. If you or your dog are facing a sheep and position yourself slight to the sheep's right as you flank around the sheep, then this will usually result in movement of the sheep to the left (away from the pressure of the handler). Occasionally a sheep with turn to watch a dog or handler and move TOWARD them, rather than away, but this would be an exception to the general rule. If you have very tame sheep or sheep that have been bottle-fed or handled a lot, they may not react to the presence of the handler in the same way that less tame sheep will. Actually moving the sheep yourself will be beneficial in learning about where to put the dog in order to influence movement of the sheep. If your sheep are very tame, using ducks for this exercise can be helpful. However, the movement of ducks can change very rapidly, so you have to be very observant and use small scale movements in order to move them where you want them to go.

When you are trying to influence the movement of sheep, you must present some energy and pressure that will result in a response. If you cannot create movement in the stock, try to determine if other people can create movement and study the way that they move and present themselves to the sheep. This is also a factor in presentation of yourself to your young dog during the early training stages. Creating movement or flanking without creating forward movement will be important to master with your dog.

If a sheep is moving to its left and you step in front of it, you will create a barrier and the sheep should stop (unless very determined to keep going!) or the sheep will turn around and go the other direction (because you are now directly in front of its eye). If you have stopped the sheep, a flanking movement with forward pressure to your right (sheep's left if you are facing the sheep) will result in counter movement of the sheep to its right. This type of movement may happen very quickly. One second you will be behind the eye, then, as the sheep moves, you may be in front of the eye, or the sheep may have crossed over and you are now behind the other eye! This will be especially noticeable with light sheep or sheep that are not accustomed to being handled. It may be harder to observe in tame sheep, but will occur with sufficient movement (pace, presence, size and degree of movement).

If the sheep are moving and you move up along the right side of a sheep from the rear, your presence will eventually cause the sheep to turn to the left. Notice where you will have to be in order to create the left turn. Usually you will NOT be directly opposite the sheep's head. If you have a goat you will have to move farther around to the head in order to achieve the same effect since a goat's eyes are set farther forward in the head and not as laterally as those of a sheep.

Likewise, sheep may have difficulty seeing directly in front without putting their heads down. Because of the lateral positioning of the eye in the head, they will more easily see the area along their side and somewhat behind them. If you want to keep a sheep moving in a straight line (for instance in a trial, to make the fetch gates), then, depending on the pressures influencing the sheep, you may have to exert pressure from behind, from the side and/or a combination of alternating pressure in both locations. That is why you may see dogs in very different locations relative to the sheep that achieve the same result. The position of the two different dogs may be different yet still achieve the same result. The difference will depend on the forces influencing sheep movement, as well as the power and presence of the dog in controlling the sheep.

Creating the Hook

Usually we think and talk about the dog moving the stock toward or away from the handler and this is the result of the stock moving away from the dog. A special circumstance that you should note and be aware of is the ability of a dog to control the sheep with the end result of slowing the sheep down or pulling them TO him by influencing the eye. You may see this occur with some dogs at a trial. The sheep may be running away from other dogs, even when the dog is at a considerable distance, but certain dogs seem to be able to magically create an invisible connection or hook between themselves and the sheep. This invisible connection between the sheep and the dog may be transient or sustained, but, when sustained and perpetuated with confidence, this results in flowing movement of the sheep that is a beautiful thing to watch!

When the Hook is Excessive

But, this type of influence may also create problems if it the connection is created, but there is not appropriate follow through by the dog to continue with the flow. As you work with your dog to develop and refine the hook, expect these problems to happen! It will be part of the process of your dog's development of the hook and confidence in his ability to control stock. Be aware that these problems are part of a phase that will need to be worked through in order to achieve the ultimate goal!

For instance, at the lift a dog may create the connection between himself and the sheep, drawing the attention of the sheep to him. If he does not continue with the lift with confidence, the sheep may actually turn and move TOWARD the dog. This can create a stand off or problem for the dog in creating forward motion of the sheep to start the sheep moving. Sometimes you may have to use short flanks to the left and/or right with forward pressure to break this sort of stand off and accomplish the lift.

This same thing may happen at the pen. If the dog has drawn the sheep to him and the sheep feels it cannot escape to either side, it may end up going over the top of the dog! This is not just the result of mesmerization that occurs with a strong-eyed dog; it tends to happen when the dog that has been creating movement of the sheep then sucks back, drawing the sheep to him. In order to remedy this situation, it may require a small flank to move the dog away from a face-to-face situation. This may be difficult to accomplish because the dog may be wary at this point since he may not have the degree of control that he feels is necessary or because the sheep consider the dog to be weak at that moment and feel that they now have the upper hand! This same situation may occur at the shed with the same kind of intense pressure that happens at the pen.

Refinement of the Hook

The refinement of the hook is the ultimate goal in creating a flowing style of working, whether on the farm or on the trial field or in the trial arena. The result of having the hook is a dog that will move the sheep smoothly and continuously with an appropriate pace and exertion of just the right amount of pressure on his flanks, when driving, fetching, shedding and penning.

INTRODUCTION TO WHISTLES

Introduction

Whistle commands are a traditional part of working herding dogs. Using whistles while working your dog is nice since you don't have to yell for your dog to hear you at a distance. The subject of whistles and variations that can be communicated is worthy of an entire text itself. This chapter will include introductory remarks about using whistles and things that you should think about when choosing whistles to use with your dog.

Choosing Whistles

You should choose whistles that are easy for you to consistently blow. Each command should be distinct and not have notes that are similar for different commands. Practice whistles on your own until you can be consistent; only then will you be ready to try to teach whistles to your dog. Try recording your whistles and then play them back to see if they sound like you think they do and should. Sometimes you will be able to recognize inconsistencies or similarities in whistles that can be confusing.

You will also have to choose the type of commercial whistle that you will use or if you will whistle with your mouth and/or fingers. A lot of people, myself included, cannot whistle using just the mouth and fingers, so whistle using a commercial whistle. There is some variation among the different types of whistles, depending on their shape and material from which they are made. Choice of a whistle will depend, in large part, on your personal preferences.

When you are first trying to blow a shepherd's whistle, don't be discouraged if you cannot immediately produce the whistles you want. If you will persevere and have patience, you will eventually be able to consistently make the whistles you want. When you can play little songs, then you will be ready to choose the whistles you will use for your commands.

Teaching Whistles

I like to start with the stop whistle first. I will teach this whistle first and not try to teach other whistles at the same time. This is a good idea if you are not accustomed to whistling to your dog. For beginners, it is easier to start with one whistle and then progressively add other whistles, one at a time, as the dog begins to respond and you become more comfortable with the whistle.

If you try to use all the whistles when you first begin, it may be too overwhelming.

After the stop whistle, I will add the walk up whistle, followed by the flanking whistles. I will give the whistle command first, followed by the verbal command. Once the dog begins responding to the whistle, I will drop the verbal command. At some point you may have to use body language and/or correction to make sure the dog is responding to the whistle without the verbal command. It is helpful to give the whistle just as the dog is 'thinking' about making the movement that you desire or stopping naturally. The timing of the whistle is very important. If you can pair it with something that the dog is thinking about doing he will go ahead and follow through with the action and is more likely to learn to associate it with the whistle than if you try and force him to respond to the whistle. If your dog does not respond to the whistle, you will have to step out and do whatever it takes to get a response. When you ask for a response, you need to make sure that response happens! This is why it is important to make sure that your whistles are clear and consistent. If you are constantly having problems with whistles while trialing or under pressure, consider whether your whistles may be reflecting pressure or if you may be coming out with a whistle that differs from that which you use at home.

You may suffer from dry mouth or slobbering when you first start using a whistle. This happens to everybody!

Variations on Whistles

You will want to have a whistle for stopping your dog, as well as for walk up, and right and left flanks. There may be subtle differences in whistles used for lie down or stand or you may choose to use two very different whistles for these commands. As you progress with your training, you will likely want a whistle for LOOK BACK, STEADY (or TAKE TIME) and to get your dog to nip on command.

When you are choosing whistles, be sure to keep in mind that you will want to have whistles that you can modify to communicate short or long flanks and to have your dog move fast or slow, depending on what you need to get the dog to do. As with your verbal commands, you will need to have distinct modifications of your basic whistles for short, regular and long flanks and to ask the dog to move fast or slow when doing these flanks.

A short flank means that the dog will move only a short distance around the stock. A long flank will make the dog move wider and travel a longer distance around the stock. Usually giving a shorter whistle or part of a two-part whistle (one tone when the regular whistle has two tones or parts) is good for a short flank. Giving a longer, more drawn out whistle will communicate that you want a longer flank. If you want the dog to go fast, repeating the whistle rapidly will usually result in faster movement. If you want the dog to go more slowly, using a softer and slower whistle is helpful.

The tone of a whistle is important. Some tones of low pitch may be hard to hear at a distance, so be aware of this when you are choosing your whistles. Some people will tell you that a whistle command will not communicate panic or emotion to a dog, as your voice can. I do not feel that this is true. You can communicate the same type of emotions with your whistles as you can with your voice. Just as you have had to consciously control the tone and volume (loudness) of your voice when working with your dog, you will have to concentrate on controlling these with your whistles. If you are constantly blowing your whistle at full volume and as hard as you can, your dog may learn to ignore softer and more subtle whistles that you will need for communicating other things to him. This is like yelling at your dog all the time!

Sometimes you will see handlers that just keep blowing whistles louder and louder if their dog does not respond to the first whistle. This may be counter productive and result in the dog expecting you to make him hear the commands. If your dog does not appear to listen to your loud whistle commands, you may have to come back to a quieter whistle in order to get him to listen. He will have to take responsibility for listening to you and hearing his commands. Sometimes the wind or terrain will make it difficult for the dog to hear your whistles at a distance. Be prepared to switch to verbal commands or blow more loudly when this happens. When working close at hand, you will have to determine if whistles or verbal commands work better for you. Sometimes sharp whistles will disturb the sheep when quiet verbal commands will not.

I imagine that I overheard a young dog as he came off the field. He laid down by an old dog and said 'Man, did you see that? I got him to repeat his commands eight times.' The old dog said, 'That's nothing, did you see how red-faced my handler got. I got him to blow harder and got him to repeat the whistle 15 times before I did what he said! He came off and complained to his friends that he had a bad headache.' Don't give your dogs that opportunity to say this about you! It may be that you need to go back to basics and use soft commands. A dog's hearing is much more sensitive than ours is!

Problems with Whistle Commands

Problems with whistles most often are because they are not clear and consistent. Give the whistle the same way each time you ask your dog to do something. Nervousness, stress or panic can cause variations in your whistles. At a trial you may be nervous and the sharpness, hardness or loudness of your whistles may change compared to what you are doing at home. It is no wonder that the dog may not respond the same since the commands are not the same. Record yourself using a small pocket tape recorder. Record yourself at home and at a trial for comparison! The same things may happen with your voice commands when you are in a strange situation, at a trial or when under stress.

Help with Whistling

A good way to find whistles that you like is to listen to accomplished handlers. If you ask them, many handlers will talk to you about their whistles and will blow them for you. There are several good tapes on whistles available commercially.

Bob training Mick on ducks

TRIALING

Introduction

Whether you use your dog for working or have a dog because you want to trial, trials can provide a way to gauge your progress in training. If approached with the right attitude and preparation, trials can be a fun and rewarding challenge for you and your dog. Don't make it a life-or-death situation. A trial is a way to measure your dog training and determine those areas that you need to work on. You can go home and make the weak places stronger and keep the strong places strong. You can then go to another trial to see if what you have been doing is working.

It is always helpful to have an expert opinion and feedback regarding what is happening with your dog in order to keep you on track. Sometimes you will not gauge what is happening correctly or are too close to see what is really happening. Sometimes you may not want to hear what someone else is saying, but it is always helpful to have someone that will tell you the truth. What is happening will not matter to the dog, as long as you are happy with him. A dog is never embarrassed. Only human beings can be embarrassed or frustrated by our lack of ability to train and handle our dogs in order to get them to do what we want. If you can find a knowledgeable person who is willing and able to help you and who knows or will come to know you and your dog, their opinion, help and advice will be invaluable!

Types of Trials

A number of organizations sanction trials in the United States. In addition, there are some trials that are not sponsored or sanctioned by organizations, but which are put on by individuals who do not seek affiliation with a particular organization.

Types of Trials Based on Sanctioning Organizations

Organizations that sanction trials include the American Kennel Club (AKC), Australian Shepherd Club of America (ASCA), American Herding Breeds Association (AHBA) and United States Border Collie Handler's Association (USBCHA). In addition, there are a variety of state or regional associations that bring together members interested in herding. You can write to these organizations and receive information about their programs, membership and trials that they hold. If you are going to trial, membership in one or more of these organizations helps support the sport in which you are involved. The more organizations and people that are involved in herding, the better it is because each group will feed into others. Don't become so narrow minded that you think one is better than another, since each has its benefits and all are needed to make the process work.

Types of Trials Based on Environment in Which They Are Held

Trials are usually classified as either Arena or Field Trials. Arena trials are held in an arena, which may vary in size from 100' x 200' or larger. The arena trial is in a smaller area than the field trial and errors are measured in inches and feet rather than yards. Arena trials usually have obstacles and pens which will be negotiated in sequence and design specified by the course. In an arena trial you may have the advantage of using a fence to help you hold the stock in position; in a field trial the dog has to contain the stock (a portable fence), as well as move them.

Field trials are held out in a field and may vary considerably as to the size and terrain. Many field trial courses are based on an international style course that has its roots and traditions in trials conducted in the United Kingdom and which have spread to all parts of the world. The parts of the international style course are those which have been covered in previous chapters in this book and include the outrun, lift, fetch, drive, pen, shed and single. Many of these elements are traditionally included in all types of herding trials. Most trials will include an outrun, lift and fetch, although the distance that the dog and stock have to travel will vary.

Types of Classes Available at Trials

The classes that are offered at trials will vary, depending on specifications of the sanctioning organization and may be based on the age of the dog and experience of the dog and/or handler. Some organizations will have a point system based on placements in various types of classes that will determine when you have to move from one type of class to another. Most of the time there will be classes that range from newly started dogs and/or handlers to those for advanced dogs and/or handlers. My advice is to enter the lowest class for which you qualify so that you and your dog can have some initial success.

Entering a Trial

Prior to entering a trial, you should do your homework. Research the various organizations that sanction trials. As a member of various organizations you will likely receive notification of trials, the type of trial, location and date. Call ahead or ask an experienced person to help you if the instructions for entry are not clear to you. Some trials will have a limit for the number of entries and a deadline by which entries should be received in order to be admitted to the trial. Some entries have to be submitted on an official entry form. Be sure to ask if this is a requirement when you contact the trial host regarding entering. Entry fees will vary.

Preparing for a Trial

You and your dog should do your best to determine what standard of performance is required prior to entering a trial. Don't expect to be able to train your dog to trial standard in a week. A rule of thumb for the inexperienced is to count on at least a year of training before attempting a trial. This may vary depending on the person and whether or not the dog has had previous training.

Go to watch some trials, if possible, before entering one yourself. This way you will have a better idea of what is expected and what you and your dog will have to do.

Make sure that you know the rules for the organization, type of trial and class that you are entering.

Be sure to take the following things with you:
1. First, make sure you have your dog!
2. A crook
3. Water for you and the dog
4. Food for yourself [some trials will have concessions]
5. A chair
6. Rule book
7. Plastic bags to clean up after your dog and to put garbage in.

You will also need a leash for your dog and a chain or cable that your dog cannot chew through if tying your dog is possible at the trial. A crate for the dog is also a good idea; if your dog is not used to being tied in a crowded situation or he becomes excited or barks when at a trial, placing him in a crate is good way to keep him calm and keep him from bothering other exhibitors and spectators. A hat or cap and sunscreen can be helpful in preventing sunburn or heat exhaustion in the summer and an umbrella or tent can be helpful in providing shade. I always pack raingear and, in most seasons, also take a coat since you never know when the weather may change.

If you are not an experienced trialer, always arrive well before the trial starts. This way you will be able to find a convenient place to park. If you can find a place that will provide afternoon shade, this can make you and your dog more comfortable. Go to the secretary or course director to get your number or running order. If it is allowed, you may be able to walk the course and familiarize yourself with how the gates open and close, where you should enter the trial arena or field and where the sheep are held and exhausted.

You will want to attend the handler's meeting. This is a meeting held prior to the start of the trial and/or prior to the beginning of separate classes. Don't be afraid to ask questions at the handler's meeting if you do not understand the instructions of the judge or the specifications for the class. Some people are afraid to ask questions; don't be afraid to ask questions—it is better to ask so that you can get the answer from the person who is judging or who is in charge of the course instead of second hand!

Make sure that you have walked your dog so that he can relieve himself and relax prior to your class. Be punctual when it is your turn to run. Determine if you will be expected to take the sheep to the exhaust pen following your run or if there is a person or dog that will be doing this. If there is a person and dog that is exhausting sheep, call your dog off and honor the work of this dog while he is taking the sheep to the exhaust pen. If you are expected to exhaust the sheep, take them directly to the exhaust pen and do not work the sheep on the way to the exhaust pen. This is not an opportunity to train your dog!

Before it is your turn to run, be sure that you have watched other people run the course. Watch how the sheep are responding, how the terrain effects the dog and the sheep, and recognize the pressures that may be pulling the sheep in a particular direction. Try to determine how the sheep are influenced in any way on the course. Take the time to visualize your own run and review your flanking commands as you visualize you and your dog on the course so that you will not be telling your dog to go one way when you actually mean for him to go the opposite way.

When it is your turn to run, be ready to move onto the course promptly, but wait until the previous dog's sheep have been exhausted. You may be required to check in with a secretary, judge or course director prior to proceeding onto the course. Once you have started the run, it is up to you and your dog. You will know that you are becoming a seasoned handler when you are able to come off the course and see the run in your head, know approximately what your score will be, and know where you and your dog had faults or good points, the degree of error involved and what you have learned from the experience. Don't worry if your initial experiences are a blur. This happens with many inexperienced handlers and will get better with time and experience. Your goal is to be able to judge your own run and know what you need to work on at home in order to improve. It sounds simple, but this may take a long time to learn!

How and What to Learn from a Trial

The first thing that you will learn is that a trial is not the same as working your dog at home! The pressure of working your dog at a different place, on different stock, in the presence of numerous people and other dogs, and in a competitive atmosphere often results in a decrease in the level of performance that you will be able to achieve compared to what you can accomplish on your home turf. Be prepared for this! Your dog will not listen as well, may seem to forget some of what he knows and will often be pushier at a trial than he is at home. You will likely give at least one wrong command or may not remember the direction you are supposed to take the stock or what comes next in the sequence of events. You may have trouble remembering your flanking commands and/or whistles. You may have a tendency to want to stop your dog in order to give yourself time to think. The sheep will not be what you are used to and may be difficult for you to read. Don't worry—all of these things are normal for inexperienced handlers. You may be embarrassed by your performance, regardless of its actual worth. Remember that everyone started out as an inexperienced handler at some point! With good preparation, concentration, visualization and a good attitude, this should be a learning experience. As you get more comfortable, everything becomes easier!

In order to learn from trials, you will want to watch as many other exhibitors as you can. Watch those in classes higher and lower than the one you are in. Just because a person is in a lower level class does not mean that you cannot learn something from them! It is helpful to study and understand the score sheets or score board; try to determine where points are being deducted and why. It is helpful to sit and mark other runs just as if you were the judge; this will help you understand the judge's job and help you concentrate on a run in a way that is not possible with casual observation while talking to your friends or fellow competitors. With the best judges, your score should be very close. But, remember, even if you do not have the same score as the judge, the order of placings should be close to or the same. Even if you differ, remember that is one person's opinion on the day and that a poor score or good score does not reflect the overall worth of a person or a dog. Some days it is just not their day to shine!

There is some value to talk and discussion among fellow competitors, particularly if the discussion is led by an experienced handler. But, be aware that many discussions do not address the factors of merit. Be selective in who you listen to since everyone has an opinion and will try to convince you that their opinion is the only right one. Be open-minded and learn to form your own opinions. Many experienced handlers will be willing to help you after they are convinced that you are serious about improving and that you value and respect their opinion and advice. This may take some time. However, be aware, that, as you improve and become more competitive, that there will be fewer and fewer handlers who are willing to help someone who has reached a level of experience and competency which may threaten their placing at a trial.

Attitude and Philosophy for Trials

If competitions are unduly stressful for you, yet you want to become better and enjoy the experience of trailing, there are multiple motivational and self-help books and tapes about competitive sports that can help you.

What you get out of trialing will depend, in large part, on your personal goals and the satisfaction you can achieve from seeing progress in you and your dog. Even if you do not have the best run, you may be able to see improvement in parts of your performance and the performance of your dog that reflect your hard work and dedication to training. But, remember that some days nothing will go right—that is just part of trailing. There is always another day and another trial! When you go to compete, don't go to beat someone else. The only person against which you have to judge yourself is yourself! If you try to beat someone else, you will end up beating yourself. Go out there to try to have the best run that you and your dog can have—that is all that matters! Once your run is over it doesn't matter any more. You can now move on and think about tomorrow. The only person who can make a trial experience miserable for you is yourself. Don't look only at the parts that you think were not right, but also see the parts that were good. Learn from these, have a training plan without excessive drilling that will destroy the foundation that you have with your dog, and move on. All that matters is that you and your dog enjoy each other's company and each and every trial.

Bob loading chute with Lynn

THE OUTRUN AND LIFT

Introduction

The outrun is when the dog leaves you side and goes around to gather the sheep. The ideal shape is said to be a pear-shaped outrun whereby the dog will leave your side at a slight angle and then gradually widen as he approaches the stock and moves around to the far side of the stock in order to be in position to bring them to you. The lift is when the dog initiates movement in the livestock. The lift should cause the sheep to move in a straight line toward the handler. It should start the sheep moving smoothly, without startling them or producing rough work. Ideally, the dog should not initiate the lift until the outrun is completed. At the end of the outrun he may stop or pause in order to assess the situation and then approach the sheep in a manner that is workman-like and demonstrates his authority and control over them.

Competition Application

Virtually all competitive trials, except some arena trails where you have to take your sheep out of a pen to start, will start with an outrun. You have to get the dog to the sheep and this is the first step. There are a variety of factors that determine the correct path for the outrun, but the goal is for the dog to get to the opposite side of the sheep without disturbing them. You will have to be able stop your dog, redirect him while he is outrunning or adjust the outrun in or out while he is on the move. The point where the outrun ends is when the dog reaches the balance point to lift his sheep straight to the handler. In competition, the handler will often stop the dog at this point with a lie down or stand command, but I like to train a dog to pause or stop himself at this point rather than relying on the handler to stop him.

It may be impossible to determine if the dog has stopped in the correct place until you see the direction of lift. If the sheep move directly toward the handler, the balance point was most likely correct; if the sheep move off at an angle or do not come directly toward the handler, this means the point where the dog stopped was not correct and he will lose points on both the outrun and the lift.

Components of the Outrun and Lift

In order to do an outrun and lift, you will have to:
1. Have a dog with enough interest in working the stock to look up the field and want to go to gather his sheep
2. Be able to position the dog on your left or right side, depending on the direction that you want to send him for the outrun
3. Be able to stop your dog
4. Be able to redirect your dog while he is outrunning
5. Be able to get your dog to WALK UP
6. Be able to read the sheep in order to keep them coming on a straight line toward you.

Teaching and Learning Various Components of the Outrun and Lift

1. *Sufficient interest in working stock*

We have previously talked about building interest in your dog (see Chapter 5, Building Interest).

An integral part of channeling this interest so that the dog can successfully do the outrun is to teach the dog to **look for his stock**. It is important that he has a good idea of where the stock are in order to do the outrun. In advanced training and competition situations he may have to run blind (not knowing where the sheep are) and have to trust the handler that is sending him to direct him, if needed, to find the sheep. In the early stages of training, however, it is important that the dog knows where the sheep are. You will have been teaching this dog to spot sheep by walking toward and looking at his stock before you send him on flanks around the stock. Keep the initial outruns short so that he can have some success. Gradually lengthen the outrun. It is helpful to stop the dog, leave him at the spot from which he will start the outrun, and walk out closer to the sheep. This will help him spot the sheep and you will be in a position to make sure that he outruns in the correct shape and that you can stop him when he gets to the opposite side of the sheep. Initially you will be closer to the sheep than the dog. Gradually you can move closer to the dog, until you are sending him from your side. This will take time. Start with a length of outrun with which you KNOW the dog will be successful and then build up to a longer outrun and outruns with challenges (difficult terrain, sheep out of sight).

Teaching him to spot sheep a longer distance away is an extension of this work. In a trial situation, you may see young dogs that focus on the sheep that are being taken to the exhaust pen and they will not focus on the sheep that are set out on the field for him to gather. You can help your dog learn to focus on the sheep out in the field rather than on sheep in a pen (like an exhaust pen) or sheep in another field by setting up these situations at home. Put some sheep in a pen at several locations at the periphery of the field and make sure that you can get your dog to run by these pens and not focus on them when you send him on an outrun to gather sheep in the field. If he does get fixated on the sheep in a pen, go to him and direct his attention to the sheep you want by walking him toward them and then flanking him again. If you have a friend you can work with, let the dog watch another dog work the sheep out on the field or see your friend move sheep into position and hold them for you to do an outrun.

You can also help your dog learn to spot sheep by directing YOUR attention to the sheep you want him to gather. Don't watch the sheep going to the exhaust pen yourself or direct your attention to other sheep. If you pay attention to them, your dog will be more likely to pick up on your interest and also direct his attention to them.

You can teach him a word to spot sheep (such as LOOK or WATCH)—this will be his cue to be looking for sheep. Observe his reactions carefully and you will be able to recognize when he spots his sheep and see the recognition register in his expression and body positioning.

Another good thing to help your dog spot his sheep and start on the outrun with the correct attitude and purpose is to make sure that you have him walk out into the field or to the handlers post at or near your side (within a 6-8' zone) and on the side to which you will be sending him. He may move a short distance ahead of you, but should not be circling, jumping or flopping around. He should be looking down the field as you approach the handler's post or place from which you are going to send him. He must learn to settle and wait until you send him since you may have to wait for the sheep to be positioned properly at a trial or for various conditions in a working situation. You should walk on a direct line straight to the sheep so that he can learn to focus down the field; don't walk at an angle where he will not be able to focus on his sheep.

It is helpful to teach the dog to set up on either side of you. You may want to start off with the dog on one side, but then should have the option of placing the dog on the other side. You may have to start off on leash and walk him up toward the sheep with him on one side of you, set him up and tell him to look for his sheep. Then pass the leash behind you and ask him to come and set up on the other side. That way he will not be advancing on his stock. After you can do this with little or no direction from the leash, try it without the leash.

Practice doing this so he does not always anticipate the direction you are going to send him. Make sure it is YOUR idea to have him switch sides and set up on the other side, not his idea. If you let him do it whenever he feels like it, you will have trouble getting him to go in a particular direction when that is your preference or mandatory (as it is in some trials).

2. Positioning Your Dog on Your Left or Right Side

You and your dog should be comfortable with the dog walking on either side of you. You can indicate to your dog the side you want him to be on by patting your leg or having a word to indicate which side you want him on.

You will need to practice this on leash and then should work up to having him walk with you when off leash or when dragging a rope. If he is not comfortable doing this off stock, it will be almost impossible for you to keep him where you want him to be when setting up to work. Some handlers will angle their dogs relative to the sheep in order to promote a wider or shallower outrun. How you set up the dog will depend on the dog and his natural tendencies and degree of comfort. You will have to figure out what you and your dog are comfortable with, but remember that this positioning can influence the path that the dog takes. If he runs too wide or square, you may want to have him start facing straight out into the field instead of an angle. If he runs tight, a slight angle may be helpful in getting him to cast out around his sheep and maintain the correct shape to his outrun.

When you send the dog from your side, the first few steps as he leaves your side will help you determine if he is thinking about going around his sheep correctly or cutting in. If you will become accomplished at reading your dog, you can stop him and use your OUT or BACK and then redirect your dog with a flank if he is cutting in, running too tight or crossing the field. If he does not take the OUT or BACK command, stop the dog and move toward him in order to enforce this command. It will take some practice to make sure that the dog will take your commands at a distance from you; up until now most of your work has been close at hand. If he does not respond, do not be lazy—go out to the dog and make sure that you enforce the command, even if he is a long distance from you. You may have to help him find his sheep if he cannot find them. This will help build his confidence in you and help him learn that when you send him there WILL be sheep for him to gather.

3. Stopping your dog on the outrun

You should not only be able to stop your dog when he reaches the top of the outrun, but at a variety of places on the outrun. The clockface exercise used with flanking (See Chapter 7 on Teaching Right and Left Flanks) provides a foundation for this time of work. A good rule of thumb is to stop your dog at the top of the outrun if he is coming onto the sheep too strong. If he naturally pauses at the top of the outrun and approaches his sheep with care, you will not need to stop him. If your dog is uncertain on the outrun and is not running enthusiastically you will not want to stop him as much on the outrun, but your goal will be able to stop your dog anywhere on the outrun. This is an important part of being able to redirect your dog on the outrun.

4. Redirecting Your Dog on the Outrun

You will need to be able to redirect your dog while he is on the outrun if he is not maintaining the correct path in order to gather his sheep. He may want to cut in or cross the course when on the trial field. You want to widen or narrow the outrun if he is going to tight or too wide. For the initial stages of training you will need to be able to stop your dog before redirecting him. In advanced training you will be able redirect your dog while he is on the run.

You will need him to stop, take a BACK and OUT, WALK UP and flank. As usual, you may have to move toward the dog or between the dog and the sheep in order to enforce your commands. You may take advantage of natural training opportunities as they arise, but also will have to make sure that you ask the dog to do these things, regardless of the situation, just because you have requested him to do them! If the dog breaks and goes out around the sheep when you are trying to correct him, it is important that you do not let him lift or handle his sheep. Stop him and then take him back to where you originally had the problem and make the correction. If you have to, put him on a rope so that you can control him and stop him. Don't expect the dog to be perfect or pick on him too much—you may destroy his confidence and enthusiasm for the outrun. Make sure that you maintain his interest in gathering his stock. You may have to tolerate minor problems and work on these a small piece at a time by influencing and redirecting him.

5. *Walking up for the lift*

After your dog has completed the outrun, you will ask him to stop. Then ask him to WALK UP. You would like him to approach the sheep in a quiet and orderly manner that allows the sheep to turn and flow in a soft movement towards you. But, young dogs often want to rush the sheep or the sheep may be startled and move off too rapidly. This creates a snowball effect, with the sheep and the dog moving progressively faster on the fetch. If you have a good lift you are more likely to be able to maintain control and have a good fetch. If you startle the sheep on the lift this may effect your entire run and you may never get the sheep settled enough to work nicely.

Sometimes wait to see if your dog will slow down on his own close to the point where you would have stopped him. See if he will begin to pause or stop himself prior to the lift and if he will walk up on the stock in a manner that will cause the sheep to move off quietly. If he does NOT do this, you will have to continue to stop him or may have to tell him to BACK or OUT if he is pushing too strongly or if he is cutting in on the outrun and creating movement of the sheep. With correct repetitions your dog should learn to do this. If he is not learning to do this over time, then there is likely a fault in your outrun or lift that you are not recognizing and which needs to be corrected.

6. *Reading the Sheep for the Outrun and Lift*

You will have to learn how to read the sheep in order to make a good outrun and lift. It may be hard to imagine how you might need to read the sheep for an outrun—but, watching the way the sheep are facing, determining which direction they prefer to move off by watching other dogs, and observing where the set-out person and dog (if using a dog) stand and how the set-out person calls off the dog will all influence the direction you will want to send your dog and how you will handle your dog for your outrun and lift. In addition, watching the reaction of the sheep as the dog approaches for the lift will determine whether you may want to remain quiet, flank him or steady him or encourage him. So, don't assume that reading your sheep applies only to when they are moving! By being able to read the amount of pressure that the dog is putting on the sheep and their reaction to it, you will be able to make appropriate adjustments. All actions are the result of intentions and thoughts of the sheep that have happened several stages before you have seen them react. If you can become good at reading your sheep you may be able to read their thoughts and intentions before they move; if you can act at this stage it is better than reacting to the actual movement. You are able to prevent things from happening, not just reacting to them after it has happened!

You also need to learn to read your dog because he will tell you what he is going to do before he does it. Dogs that have a tendency to grip under pressure may yawn, drool, pick up one ear, lower in front or bounce before gripping. If you can see these preliminary signs, you may be able to prevent the grip. So, reading your stock and your dog is very important for the outrun and the lift, as well as during other aspects of work.

Problems With the Outrun

A variety of problems can occur with the outrun. This section will cover many of the common problems and how I address these.

Crossing Over

There are several reasons why a dog may cross over, also called crossing the course. It may be because you have asked a young dog to go farther than he is ready to go. It may be because the sheep have changed the direction that they are facing and the dog changes direction to go to their heads. It may be because the terrain draws him in and across. Some dogs that are very keen and overly excited to get to the sheep may run out a bit and run up the middle and through the stock, crossing the course as part of this. All of these problems require going back and working shorter outruns and gradually then lengthening out. You may have skipped some of the basics because a dog has been natural about outrunning; now is the time to go back and make sure that you have all the basics. Some people end up on a dial-a-HOPE program (1-800-HOPE), whereby they hope it gets right pretty soon. This attitude will not get you very far. You need to take action. Stop the dog, walk out and keep him from crossing the course. The appropriate correction will likely involve an OUT or BACK and then a redirecting flanking command. The actual correction is not the hard part; the hard part is finding conditions and situations that will challenge your dog and in which these types of problems will show up. Only by encountering these will you be able to make the necessary corrections and teach your dog how to handle a variety of types of terrain and situations. You will need to haul your dog to as many locations and find as many types of sheep to work as possible in order to provide him with a well balanced education.

Running Too Tight

This problem may manifest itself as running too tight over the entire outrun or just at the top of the outrun. This can be caused by the dog being on the wrong lead. You will have to go back and work on the basics of flanking with stops and backing up, turning him over himself in the direction you want to go. This will help him flank and get the correct lead. Usually he will widen out on his own when he begins to take the correct lead. You can also stop the dog, make him take an OUT and flank him immediately after the OUT without stopping him. If he does not take the OUT, you will have to stop him, have him OUT, stop him again and then flank him.

Another common reason for running too tight is that the dog is anticipating moving the sheep. If the dog is running too tight at the top of the outrun, you will have to place yourself close to the sheep so you can walk through them and push him out at the top of the outrun. If you fix it at the top of the outrun, it will often result in him giving more room on the side of the outrun, too. Don't let him handle the sheep each time he completes his outrun; let him lift the sheep only every 2nd or 3rd time he does the outrun to keep him from thinking only about moving the sheep.

Flat on the Top of the Outrun

A lot of dogs get flat on the top of the outrun because they will see some movement of the sheep as they pass them and they will come in because they think the sheep are going to get away. Other dogs will be flat at the top of the outrun because they have not learned to keep rounded flanks. If the sheep do not stay in place while the dog completes his outrun this can also cause a dog to flatten out at the top since he is moving to follow the sheep as they head for the handler or run away.

For the first two problems, I'll work on flanking the dog to the top. If he starts to flatten out or turn in, stop him, ask him to OUT and flank him again. If he does not take the OUT, you will have to walk toward him and enforce the OUT. Do not worry about the sheep at that moment. Get the dog to finish what you've asked him to do. You can always flank him back in the opposite direction to get him to retrieve the sheep. But, a good way to keep sheep in one place for these problems and for the third problem (sheep leaving the spot before the outrun is completed), you can tie two sheep up and leave one free. That way the sheep will be there when he arrives and you do not have to worry about them running away. If you have a friend that will hold the sheep, this is an alternative way to keep the sheep in one place.

Do not let the dog move the sheep every time he does an outrun. You may have to stand closer to the sheep in order to keep them from running down the field toward you. But, your best bet is to have somebody hold them for you, go to a lot of places to work your dog with someone to hold the sheep. This way your dog learns that the sheep will be there when he arrives. If you let this problem continue it will be very difficult for your dog to learn how to have a good lift.

Running Too Wide (Running off contact)

It may sometimes be difficult to tell the difference between just wide enough and too wide. In other instances it is obvious when a dog is running too wide and has lost contact with his sheep. This is a matter of degree and depends on the dog and the reaction of the sheep. If the dog is running and knowing where his sheep are and the sheep are aware of the dog, this dog is in contact. Another dog may run the exact same path but be too wide and not have contact or communication with his stock. This dog will have to be stopped at the top in order to be told where his sheep are. If left on his own, this dog may run on past the sheep and end up going all the way around the field. With the dog that is running wide but with contact, the dog may overrun slightly, but will end up finding his sheep. The dog that is in contact will periodically check on his sheep as he is running—what I call checking in. This may be a slight turn of the head over his shoulder or may be noticeable only by the muscle tension and attitude of the dog as he is running. To address the problem of running too wide/off contact, I'll send the dog on his outrun. The minute that I notice that he is going too wide (this may be virtually as he leaves your feet), I will stop him and then walk him directly toward the sheep until I see that he has re-established contact with them. Then I will flank him again. If he goes too wide again, I'll stop him again and then repeat this. Soon he may begin anticipating stopping and walking up to the sheep. He may look at the sheep more as he realizes that he is going around the sheep, not just running to the other side and relying on the handler to tell him where the sheep are. If he then wants to come in and run too tight, you can always give him an OUT and get him to run a bit wider. It is usually easier to push them out than it is to bring them in.

Another way to try to keep the dog from running too wide is to use a HERE, HERE. But, this can be used only when the dog is aware of his sheep and paying attention to them. The HERE, HERE will have the effect of bringing him back towards his sheep. You may have to add a flank to keep him on the path of the outrun if he hesitates wants to come straight toward the sheep. By doing these things you should be able to either widen or narrow your outrun.

Even if your dog does not have a problem with running too wide or too tight, it is important that you practice being able to do these things.

As the dog gains experience, this seems to help dogs learn to check in, read their stock and widen out (bubble out) so they do not disturb the sheep as they go around them. It is a beautiful thing to watch a dog make these kinds of move in response to the handler or on his own.

Hesitating or Stopping on the Outrun

Sometimes a dog will develop the problem of hesitating or stopping on the outrun. This may be caused by a lack of confidence. Sometimes the dog is fearful of going around strange dogs and/or people and is hesitant to go around the set-out person and/or set-out dog. The best way to help this is to work the dog in the presence of strange people and dogs doing the set-out. Do this on relatively short outruns so that you can get the dog to get over this. You may have to encourage the dog with a shh-shh-hh or an additional flanking command to keep him going. Soon the dog will get more comfortable and this problem will likely gradually disappear. Occasionally there will be a dog that this continues to bother, but you can get them to do the outrun without hesitating or stopping because they trust you and your judgment.

If it is unrelated to the people at the top of the field, you may have to encourage your dog to keep running with a shh-hh or additional flanking command. If your dog is asking for help and to be re-assured, it is not a crime to do this. Don't do this without reason, but don't neglect to do it if he needs it. Again, shorten the outrun to start so that he will gain confidence. You may have to get close enough to sheep so that the dog can see you as you encourage him to go on around. Then lengthen the outrun gradually as he improves on the shorter outruns. Don't be in a hurry to stretch out the outrun.

Stopping Short on the Outrun

Stopping short on the outrun refers to the dog that does not go all the way to the point of balance but stops short of this point. This will result in a lift that pushes the sheep off line and in a direction that is not directly toward the handler. This may be the result of a dog feeling pressure from the sheep when they are facing him on the outrun. Dogs that are more difficult to flank have a tendency to stop short on the outrun. You have to get both of these types of dogs moving more freely on their flanks. You will need to flank them all the way around the sheep or 1 and 2 times around. Then flank them back to the place where they should have stopped. Sometimes you may think that a dog has stopped short, but, when he makes the lift, you find that the lift will be directly to you. This dog has made the correct judgment. If you start flanking him past this point, you may communicate that he was wrong and he'll soon stop stopping on his own and quit using his own judgment and natural ability to read the pressure.

Over-running on the Outrun

When a dog over-runs on the outrun, this means that he has run past the point of balance. Just as with stopping short, this will result in a lift that is off line and which does not move the sheep directly toward the handler.

Most dogs that I see that over-run are those that are easy and fluid to flank. When people do not allow the dog to feel the balance point and practice letting him use his judgment to find balance, it is easy to get this type of dog to move too far past the balance point. He may become reluctant to walk up and apply pressure. When flanking this type of dog when he is close at hand, you will need to help him learn where to turn in on his stock by telling him 'there' and letting him walk onto his stock and move them toward you as you step away from the stock. If you have him do some driving, this will also help him develop some more push. Be sure that you have him move the stock more than you flank him.

Dog Leaves the Handler's Side Too Square

Sometimes you will see a dog that leaves the handler's side at a 90 degree angle or actually runs at an angle that takes him behind the plane of the handler as he starts his outrun. This may occur with the dog that runs too wide and off contact, but some dogs that do not run too wide for the entire outrun will start their outrun this way. This is a fault because it wastes ground, time and energy and does not result in the dog concentrating on his stock. Some dogs will naturally break wide and run this way. Other dogs develop this because they have been pushed out to widen the outrun and feel that if they break wide or run to the fence that they are doing what we want. Sometimes the dog will have to run all the way to the fence to give sufficient room, but they should run forward and out to the fence, not at a right angle or breaking behind the handler as they leave his/her side. So, when you push your dog out, remember to push him out when he is close to the livestock, not at the start of the outrun. When you are pushing him out, do it when it is needed, but don't let it become a habit. If you see the dog doing this on his own, don't let it become a habit. Change the way that you are working him. If he starts to do this, stop him, walk him up toward the sheep as for the correction for running too wide (see the previous section). If he breaks too far out again, stop him and repeat this again until he realizes that you want a flank that moves him forward and out, not backwards and out.

Getting Lost on the Outrun or Running Blind

Some dogs will get lost on the outrun. Running blind refers to the dog running on the outrun when he is not able to see his sheep for all or part of the outrun. Getting lost is relatively common in young dogs or in situations where the dog may lose track of where the sheep or may have part or all of the outrun that is blind (where he cannot see his sheep as he is running). A lot of dogs get lost because they haven't had enough experience to find sheep on their own. You will need to start practicing these types of situations. Start out with an outrun in which he will have to go over a ditch or a few rolling hills without seeing his sheep. I like to be able to see the dog so that I can help direct him to the area where the sheep are. This is most easily accomplished running on the side of a hill with rolling terrain. The dog will have times when he is running blind, but you will be able to see him as he runs up the side of the hill. Start off with less complicated outruns and progress to more difficult ones. Don't overface the dog to begin with. The more practice you can provide for your dog to learn to do this, the better. As they become more proficient at this I believe that they are learning to use all their senses (sight, hearing and smell) to help them find the sheep. This is a place where you will have to be able to redirect your dog in order for him to find the sheep. You will likely need to be able to stop, OUT or BACK your dog, flank and LOOK BACK. You may have to widen your dog or bring him in as he outruns. All of these commands should be practiced in order to direct your dog to sheep that he cannot always see.

Concluding Remarks

If you cannot get to the sheep you will have no chance at being judged around the trial course or getting the sheep to the barn. That is why an outrun is important! If the dog cannot lift the sheep, then he also cannot fetch them. If the lift is not done calmly and quietly, the sheep will be disturbed, may not settle and may be difficult to move. Lots of repetition in many places, in different terrain and with different types of sheep will be needed. The more opportunities you can give your dog to practice correct outruns and lifts, the better he will become. If your practice is sloppy, then the end result will never improve. Practice these correctly in order to instill good habits in yourself and your dog.

Mick, the Kelpie, working sheep

THE FETCH

Introduction

The lift flows into the fetch, once movement of the sheep has been initiated. The fetch should be toward the handler. If you are in a competition situation or standing at a gate, the fetch should be in a straight line toward the handler. If you are moving, the dog should hold the sheep to you, whatever line you are walking. Ideally the sheep should be walking or trotting, not running full out for the fetch. Sometimes the sheep will come fast, regardless of the dog, but the best situation for your sheep and the dog is usually not at speed. If the sheep deviate from the line that will bring or hold the sheep to the handler, you may have to help him by flanking. But, your goal is to teach your dog to make these adjustments automatically without you telling him to do so.

Competition Application

Many types of competitions will require the dog to bring the sheep through a set of gates (fetch panels) set on either side of a straight line from where the sheep have been set out to the handler's post. Some trials may not have fetch panels, but you will still need to bring the sheep in a straight line to you. The fetch ends half way around the turn around the handler's post. After the sheep are half way around the post, you are beginning the drive.

Components of the Fetch

The components of the fetch and basic tools which you may need in order to fetch include:

1. Walk up
2. Holding a line
3. Pacing the sheep on the fetch
4. Flanking on the fetch
5. Stopping on the fetch
6. Out and Back
7. Turning around the post

1. Walking Up on the Fetch

You dog must walk up when asked in order to lift the sheep and to bring them on the fetch. If your dog will not walk up when asked, it is likely that the fetch will be stop-and-start or your dog may lose control of the sheep because he is not maintaining constant pressure and contact.

2. Holding the Line on the Fetch

Your dog will need to be able to exert sufficient pressure on the sheep to hold the line of the fetch. There is a delicate balance between exerting too much pressure and pushing the sheep too fast or off line and being able to flank your dog or have him walk up and still have him exert sufficient pressure to hold the sheep on the line that you desire. Sometimes the dog will have to be positioned off to one side or the other of the sheep in order to hold them on line.

3. Pace on the Fetch

The dog will have to pace the sheep on the fetch. If he is pushing too strongly or does not hook onto his sheep in order to influence their eye and keep them in control, he may not be able to effectively control the speed of the sheep on the fetch. The pace is important in establishing control of the sheep, maintaining that control and setting up for the turn around the post.

Sometimes the sheep will come rapidly down the field due to no fault of the dog; in this situation you may not be able to establish the pace and control that you may prefer. However, you should be able to position your dog so that he can be ready to move or turn the sheep without allowing them to escape.

4. Stopping on the Fetch

Just as in other aspects of your work, the ability to stop your dog when and where you ask is important. Without a good stop you will not have the control to move the dog and fetch the sheep in a workman-like manner.

5. Flanking on the Fetch

The ability to flank your dog on the fetch is important in being able to hold sheep on the line of the fetch. It is important that the dog does not completely let go of the pressure when flanking; he should be able to flank and exert pressure on the sheep at the same time. He should flank far enough to the side in order to catch the eye of the sheep, but should not flank so far around that he turns the sheep back. He should flank to the side and hold that side without falling back in behind the stock unless you ask him to. He will have to be able to take a rapid series of commands, including flanks while fetching sheep that are moving rapidly. You will have to practice this at home in order to be able to handle this when at a trial or in a strange locations.

6. Back and Out

You may need a BACK or OUT in order to correct your dog or widen your dog's flanks on the fetch. Don't forget to use these if you need them. Just because the sheep are coming to you, don't forget to make sure that the dog is correct in his work.

7. Turn Around the Post

The turn around the post is an important part of starting the drive. It demonstrates the power of the dog and its ability to hold the sheep to the handler, as well as the ability to turn the sheep tightly and with a high degree of control. If the sheep become unsettled during the turn, it will be more difficult to start the drive and have a good drive. Setting up the turn around the post is often neglected. Sometimes you will want to practice having the sheep settle in front of you before making the turn; while other times you will need to practice turning without stopping. You do not need to have a post in order to practice making these types of turns!

Problems with the Fetch, Pushing Too Hard

A common problem that you will see on the fetch is the dog that pushes the sheep too hard. This may have its start with a lift that crowds and unsettles the sheep, or may occur at any time during the fetch. There is a fine line between staying in contact with the sheep and exerting sufficient pressure and pushing too hard.

In order to help correct this, you can have the dog lie down to break the pressure, but will need to IMMEDIATELY get him back up. As soon as his elbows hit the ground he will have to be back on his feet and walking up. You may have to ask him to BACK or OUT in order to correct him if he is pushing too hard. You should teach your dog to slow down using STEADY or TAKE TIME. If he does not check his speed when you give these commands, be sure that you step in and make sure that you get a response. Remember that you have the responsibility for setting the tone of the fetch—it is your responsibility to stay calm and relaxed in order to promote this in your dog and sheep. The softer and quieter you become, the softer and quieter the dog will become. You may still have to correct him for over-pushing, but be sure that you do not yell—do this in a quiet way.

If you see tension building, you may need to stop your dog, call him off and let him relax in order to break the cycle of building tension and escalating volume and frequency of commands. After a BACK or OUT, you may want to stop the dog, have him lie quietly for a period of time and then start again.

This is helpful in teaching him not to anticipate your commands and in keeping the atmosphere relaxed.

Flanking Problems on the Fetch

Several problems may occur with flanking on the fetch. One common problem is that the dog will refuse to take the flank. Other problems include the dog that flanks into the sheep or the dog that flanks so far around to the heads of the sheep that they stop or turn back. You may want the dog to flank and hold a side, but he may flank a short distance and then fall back in behind the sheep.

These problems may occur because the dog has been allowed to constantly handle his sheep on his own and he thinks he knows what you want—to bring the sheep to you. He is not allowing you to take charge and tell him how to do this. Many times this dog will not stop or flank when asked to do so. Some people may think that the dog cannot hear, and shout louder at him. The dog hears you, but chooses not to listen. You may have to go out and make him realize that you are talking to him and that you mean what you say!

The dog that flanks into the sheep is one that, when he hears the flank command, will go slightly to one side, but will dive into the sheep or push them harder. He may be reacting to the sound of your flank without thinking about what you have said. He may move forward when he hears the flank or may take the wrong flank. You will have to go back and do some basic flanking work, starting with the sheep standing still and close at hand, and then progressing to flanking while the sheep are moving and while they are at a distance from the handler.

If the dog is taking the flank and flanks around to head the sheep, resulting in them stopping or turning back, he may not be comfortable staying in the pocket on the fetch and is worried about the sheep escaping. You will want to have the ability to flank the dog to the heads of the sheep and stop them, but do not want the dog to do this on his own or when you have not asked him to do so.

You may have to go back to basics and have him flank around his sheep, and start bringing them to you. Then stop him. Make him stay lying down while the sheep move away. This will help him understand that it is okay for the sheep to leave and that this is what you want. If he is not comfortable with the sheep leaving him and moving away, he will likely also be uncomfortable with driving.

After the sheep have moved away, walk around to the same side of the sheep as the dog, and send him out around in order to widen his flank and give him an opportunity to get behind his sheep again. If the sheep moved some distance away, you may have to walk past the dog and send him on a widening path several times before he travels the entire distance to the sheep. Then I will allow him to fetch the sheep a short distance, stop him and repeat the exercise again. As the dog becomes more comfortable, I will allow him to fetch greater distances.

Problems with Pace

Pushing too hard is one problem with pace. Other problems also occur. These may include having the sheep stop and graze or stop and face the dog on the fetch. If the sheep want to stop and graze, this may be because the dog is not applying sufficient, continuous pressure to keep them moving. Or, the handler may be stopping and starting the dog because he is afraid that he may lose control of the dog and/or sheep. You will need to practice having your dog walk up and present more pressure. You will need to help him keep moving, stay on his feet and apply constant pressure, without hesitating or holding back in a way that will release the pressure. You may have to practice having him keep going—this may move the sheep more rapidly than you would ideally desire, but will help him learn to keep going. You should practice having him go at a faster speed, then slow him down. At first do not have him go at a faster speed for long periods since he will not be comfortable at speed. Let him come back down to the slower speed at which he is comfortable for a short time and then ask him to speed up again. If you keep him in a situation where he is uncomfortable, he will likely begin to resent the situation and you will lose the ability to make him respond or have a deterioration in the dog's attitude and willingness to respond. This same concept applies to slowing the dog down—ask for him to move out of his comfort zone for a very short period of time (a few steps only at first), then allow him to move back into his comfort zone for a short time before asking him to move out of his comfort zone again.

To encourage him to speed up and keep going, you may need to give short flanks followed by WALK UP in rapid succession. Don't worry too much about line, just worry about him learning to keep pushing. It is likely that he will slow down on his own at first. As he becomes more comfortable, he will more easily push and move at a faster speed for longer periods of time. This will also help you and the dog become more comfortable with sheep that are moving at a faster speed.

You will need to make sure he can make a smooth transition from pushing and moving fast to keeping the pressure on and moving slowly. It will take some time for you to be able to move your dog through his gears from fast to slow and back again with some transitions.

If the sheep turn and face the dog on the fetch, this may be because the dog has moved up on the side of the sheep and influences the eye of the sheep or the dog is not continuing to apply pressure. Some sheep will challenge the dog without apparent reason. You will have to be able to ask your dog to walk directly up to the sheep's head. As he walks he will reach a place where he will be very slow or stopped and leaning on the stock. Don't be in a hurry. If the dog is inexperienced, I may walk beside the dog and encourage him to take a nip (not a prolonged grip) on the nose of the sheep. Choose a word that you will use to get him to nip. Once he nips the nose of the sheep, make sure that he will stop and stand without flying around or flanking. He should be ready to step back and hold the pressure or cover his sheep. If he goes forward as he nips, the sheep may go out to the side and go around him and escape.

A lot of times, if you can keep your dog leaning over his front legs and putting pressure on the sheep, the sheep will realize that he is not going to give ground and will walk off.

Many people do not want to teach their dogs to nip since a dog can be excused for gripping in a trial. However, a correct nip and let go may not be penalized if the judge thinks it is justified. It is usually an incorrect grip—on the side or tail, or one where the dog holds on—that is a problem. The incorrect grip will become less frequent if you will teach your dog to nip on command because he will learn to nip only when you ask him to do so. By teaching him that he has the ability to nip when needed, you will also be building the dog's confidence in his ability to control sheep. The dog that does not realize he has the ability to nip will not have the same degree of confidence and authority.

Floating With the Sheep While Fetching

This is a common problem. You will see a dog flank out to the side in order put the sheep back on line. But, instead of the sheep going back on line, they will continue to drift or move off line with the dog staying or floating off to the side. The sheep and dog are moving parallel and the sheep are in control of the direction, instead of the dog. This will often happen with a dog that is doing a number of other things right—he is usually not pushing too hard or trying to head the sheep. He is often just behind the eye or not exerting enough pressure on the sheep to bring them back onto line. This may be recognized on the fetch, but also on the drive where the sheep continue to drift toward the dog and the dog goes with the drift. This likely has been happening at home but may not be easily noticed; it is most often recognized when you miss a gate at a trial!

In order to help this problem, you will need to flank the dog on a little bit so that he can influence the eye and turn the sheep a little and then ask him to WALK UP. Then drive a short way in the direction that you have turned the sheep. If you will be observant and correct this fault as soon as you are aware of it, it will take fewer corrections than if it has gone on for a long period of time.

The Change-of-Fetch Exercise

This is an exercise that you can do periodically to determine if you have control and flanks on the fetch with appropriate pressure that will prevent 'floating.' When the dog is bringing the sheep toward you, you will flank him to one side so that he turns the sheep at a right angle to the fetch line. Go a short distance along this line, then flank him back behind the sheep so they are again fetching toward you, but on a line parallel to that of their original path. Then flank him around to the side so that the sheep turn at a right angle and move them back to the original fetch line. When they reach this line, then flank the dog back behind the sheep again and bring them on down the fetch line. This exercise will help make sure that the fetch does not become a habit that is on automatic pilot. You should have a dog that will fetch naturally and on a straight line, but you should also be able to ask the dog to change what he is doing if you so desire!

Problems with Turning Around the Post

A variety of problems can occur when turning around the post. These include a turn that is too wide or a turn that is too narrow, often with sheep going on each side of the post. The dog may throw himself off the sheep and go too wide, may start the turn on his own, or may turn the sheep back so they are going the wrong direction. The turn around the post may be influenced by the environment (nearby fences, cars, people or other dogs). The way the handler sets up the turn and moves as the dog turns has a big influence on how the turn is conducted.

Before you want to start practicing or doing much turning, you will need to have the dog bring the sheep to you and have the sheep and dog settle out in front of you. When you start this, you may have to put some pressure on the sheep(stepping in front of them, moving toward them and/or using your crook in a swinging motion to block their path) and/or dog (OUT or BACK) so that the sheep will arrive and stay between the two of you. The sheep should be a short distance away from you, not crowding at your feet. The distance that the sheep are away from you will depend on the distance at which they will settle. You want the dog to think about settling the sheep in front of you before the sheep arrive. If you have sheep that are coming very rapidly and which want to run right past you, you will have to flank the dog to their heads and bring them back to you. This makes it very difficult to teach the task of settling the sheep. If you can, start with sheep that will move moderately easily, but not want to run past the handler.

Boxing the Post

After the sheep have settled, decide which way you want to turn them around the post. If you want them to come around on your right side, you will take one step to your left—this opens up the path for the sheep to come to the right side of the post and helps block the sheep from coming on that side. Then, have the dog walk up and bring them past you. As they move toward you and past you to go around the post, you will turn your shoulders and body to follow this movement—in other words, you will turn your left shoulder toward your dog and then rotate to follow the sheep around. If the sheep are good, the dog may likely be out to the side and slightly behind the sheep. If the sheep are trying to run or stray off line, this will influence how far around the sheep he flanks in order to hold them on line. As the sheep pass the line where the fetch is completed (half way around the post), then you should be facing along the line of the drive and ready to move the sheep toward the first set of drive panels. This movement is very important—don't take root at the post! You can move around it within a short distance from it.

After you get where you can make a turn at a slow pace, you will have to practice making the turn with sheep that are only slightly settled and sheep that are moving moderately fast. Make sure that you practice turning both directions around the post.

Common Problems

Turn Too Wide

This can occur when the sheep approach the post off line. This may be the fault of the handler or because the dog has decided to start the turn on his own. It doesn't take long before dogs will learn to anticipate the turn and may initiate this without you being aware of it! Some wide turns will be the result of the dog anticipating the place the sheep want to go (i.e., the exhaust pen) and going to cover pressure in this location without paying attention to where the sheep are. If the pressure drawing the sheep is strong to the side opposite of that which you want to turn, the dog may have to flank so far to this side that, by the time, the sheep have started around the turn, he has a tremendous amount of ground to cover in order to contain his sheep. Skillful handling of the dog when the sheep are wanting to break out or around the post may require stopping the dog and flanking the dog across the path that the sheep will take on the drive. This will result in a deduction of points, but may be preferable to losing the sheep to the exhaust pen. If everyone has lost the sheep by trying to pass them around the post, a turn in front of the post may allow you to maintain control. This will result in a large point deduction since the turn around the post is treated as an obstacle, but may be preferable to losing the sheep. These types of salvage moves are not recommended except in exceptional circumstances. Experience and observation of many handlers, dogs and sheep will be required to judge the best ways to turn around the post and what is appropriate for various types of sheep and situations!

Turn Too Narrow

This may occur if the sheep are too close to the handler before starting the turn or the handler or dog initiate a flank too soon (before the sheep are a sufficient way around the post). If you will go back to basics and learn to settle the sheep out in front of the handler, this will help keep the turn from being too narrow and having sheep split on both sides of the post. The handler should also be aware of holding his/her side of the post and blocking the sheep or putting pressure on them to help to get them to turn.

Environmental Effects

Environmental factors that influence the sheep, dog and handler at the turn around the post include the presence of people, vehicles, other dogs, fences, or objects (such as a pen or other things). Some sheep may be used to being handled and subjected to outside influences; other sheep may be more afraid or influenced by the handler than the dog, or may be more awkward around obstacles, fences or other types of pressure. Being able to read the reactions of the sheep and figuring out what things are exerting the most pressure on them will be important. This is where the turn around the post becomes a real challenge and test of your dog's ability to push, cover and read the pressure of the sheep. This is why providing opportunities for your dog to learn to do this are so important. Awkward situations for turning around the post may benefit from exercises designed to help him learn to hold sheep, step back and cover when they break and to flank quickly or slowly, depending on the need. You may have to move at a greater distance from the post or around the sheep in order to get them to move (remaining aware that there may be a point deduction if you stray too far from the post).

A smooth transition into the drive is important in starting the sheep on the correct line to the drive gates or to where-ever you want to take them. A good turn around the post will provide a good start for the drive.

Concluding Remarks

Keeping the basics sound so that you will have a dog that consistently will fetch correctly is a life long pursuit. You may think that your dog is trained to fetch, but continually refining and improving this is important. It is important to allow the dog to fetch, using his own initiative and natural ability and without handler requests or interference. It is equally important to be able to ask him to flank or stop and to do things fast or slow. Only by practice over a long period of time without nagging or drilling your dog can the balance between natural work and command be achieved. There is a fine line between allowing the dog to do his job using his own natural ability and initiative and you interfering with the dog by asking him to flank, stop, or change direction. If you see a problem developing, by all means fix it! Then let the dog do his job.

THE DRIVE

Introduction

Driving is moving the sheep away from the handler or in a direction that is not to the handler. In a competition situation, the drive starts as the sheep move half way around the post. Basic components of and tools that you will use on the drive are:

1. Walk Up
2. Line
3. Pace
4. Flanks
5. Stop
6. Back and Out
7. Turns around gates
8. Setting up for the Shed or Pen

Components of the Drive

1. Walk Up

In order to drive, you dog will have to be able to walk up. Your dog must walk up when asked in order to move the sheep on the drive. If your dog will not walk up when asked, it is likely that the drive will be stop-and-start or your dog may lose control of the sheep because he is not maintaining constant pressure and contact.

2. *Holding the Line on the Drive*

Your dog will need to be able to exert sufficient pressure on the sheep to hold the line of the drive. There is a delicate balance between exerting too much pressure and pushing the sheep too fast or off line, and being able to flank your dog or have him walk up and still have him exert sufficient pressure to hold the sheep on the line that you desire. Sometimes the dog will have to be positioned off to one side or the other of the sheep in order to hold them on line.

3. *Pace on the Drive*

The dog will have to pace the sheep on the drive. If he is pushing too strongly or does not hook onto his sheep in order to influence their eye and keep them in control, he may not be able to effectively control the speed of the sheep. The pace is important in establishing control of the sheep, maintaining that control and setting up for turns around the drive gates.

Sometimes the sheep will be moving rapidly due to no fault of the dog; in this situation you may not be able to establish the pace and control that you may prefer. However, you should be able to position your dog so that he can be ready to move or turn the sheep without allowing them to escape.

4. *Stopping on the Drive*

Just as in other aspects of your work, the ability to stop your dog when and where you ask is important. Without a good stop you will not have the control to move the dog and drive the sheep in a workman-like manner.

5. *Flanking on the Drive*

The ability to flank your dog on the drive is important in being able to hold sheep on the line of the drive. It is important that the dog does not completely let go of the pressure when flanking; he should be able to flank and exert pressure on the sheep at the same time. He should flank far enough to the side in order to catch the eye of the sheep, but should not flank so far around that he turns the sheep back. He should flank to the side and hold that side without falling back in behind the stock unless you ask him to. He will have to be able to take a rapid series of commands, including flanks, while driving sheep that are moving rapidly. You will have to practice this at home in order to be able to handle this when at a trial or in a strange locations.

6. Back and Out

You will need a BACK or OUT in order to correct your dog or widen your dog's flanks on the drive. Don't forget to use these if you need them. Just because the sheep are moving away from you, don't forget to make sure that the dog is correct in his work.

7. Turns Around Gates

In competitions, turns around gates or other obstacles should be tight. This means that the path that the sheep take should remain close to the gate or obstacle and that the turn should move the sheep directly onto the line to the next obstacle. A good turn is important in maintaining the flow of a run. The tightness of the turn will depend, in part, on the flightiness of the sheep and their speed and position as they go through the gates.

8. Setting Up for the Shed/Split or Pen

The final leg of the drive will be followed by a shed/split or by penning the sheep. This leg of the drive should be used to set up the sheep for the shed/split or the pen. For the shed or split, this will include determining whether the sheep will need to group and settle in the shedding ring or whether they can be lined out to approach and come into the ring in preparation for calling the dog in. If the pen is the obstacle that follows the last leg of the drive, you will want to be able to bring the sheep to the pen in a manner that will encourage them to look into the pen and to keep them from slipping around the pen.

Problems with Driving

Problems in Pushing the Sheep off the Handler

Refer to the Chapter on Teaching the Drive for teaching the dog to push the sheep away for the drive.

Dog Does Not Take Flanks While Driving—Refer to the Chapter on Teaching Flanks. The dog will primarily be taking inside flanks while driving (the dog is between the sheep and the handler).

Dog Looks Back at the Handler While Driving—Looking back at the handler may be the result of getting after the dog when you are located behind him or constantly asking him to stop and flank. He may be more worried about what you want him to do than he is about concentrating on his stock. This is a common problem because we tend to concentrate on moving him left and right because of anticipation or fear that the stock will escape or in order to practice going through or turning around gates or obstacles. If you constantly do this, you take away the dog's responsibility for watching the stock and positioning himself relative to them. You will have to trust your dog and allow him to drive, without worrying too much about the precision of the drive. You will need to practice letting your dog drive without interference, while walking with him, as well as moving your dog with commands during the drive.

Sometimes the dog will be confused and not understand that you want him to drive. He may hesitate or look back for help and re-assurance. You can help him by walking with him at a distance that he is comfortable with while driving. The distance that you will be will depend on the dog—you may be directly beside him or beside and slightly behind him. As he becomes more comfortable, the distance between you and the dog can be increased. Or, you may need to give him a WALK UP command in order to keep him from stopping and looking back at you. Give him the command before he stops and looks back—this may require a frequent command to re-assure him. This is one situation where frequent commands may be needed!

Dog Pushing Too Hard on the Drive—Some dogs may push too hard on the drive. This may result in sheep moving too fast, dropping sheep (see next section) or loss of control. The correction is the same as we have described for other sections on pushing too hard for the fetch.

Dropping Sheep on the Drive—Dropping a sheep refers to the dog letting one sheep separate and hold back from the rest. He will often continue to work the rest of the sheep and leave this sheep behind. This is often the result of the dog that moves up to influence the eye of a sheep that is in the front of the group. This may result in slowing of a sheep in the back and cause it to drop away from the other sheep. You will need to flank you dog back behind this sheep to tuck it back in. If needed, you will then flank him back up to hold the pressure on the front sheep. But, be aware that you have a sheep which is sensitive to the dog's movements because he may tend to drop back again. If you allow this sheep to get too far back and then try to flank the dog to tuck him in, an inexperienced dog may flank between this sheep and the rest of the group and leave him behind. Sometimes the inexperienced dog will flank into the sheep that is hanging back and grip. This is usually the result of waiting too long to tuck this sheep back in. The best cure for this is prevention! Learn to read your sheep!

Dog Floating with the Sheep on the Drive—Refer to the section on the dog floating with the sheep on the fetch in Chapter 17, The Fetch and Chapter 18, The Drive.

Sheep That Break and Run During the Drive—Sometimes, because of certain pressures that are not necessarily the fault of the dog, the sheep will break and run during the drive. This also may occur on the fetch. Usually lying your dog down will not improve the situation unless he is contributing to the problem by pushing too hard. It will likely be better to keep your dog in contact and be ready to flank him to catch the sheep if they are going off line or trying to leave the course. You may need to be able to flank your dog up the side of the sheep to catch the eye of the leaders and then back behind the sheep if you do not want to shut them down. This may all be occurring at considerable speed. You will have to practice moving at speed with your sheep and dog. The dog should still flank accurately and should not push too hard when doing this; although he will have to be coming forward to stay in contact with the sheep, the flanks should be rounded and not contribute to increasing forward momentum of the sheep. Refer to the section on the Dog Pushing Too Hard on the Fetch in the Chapter on The Fetch.

Missing Gates and Gate Problems—There may be a number of reasons why you miss the gate. Sometimes even the best handlers will misjudge either the dog or the sheep. But, if you can learn to read your sheep and keep from getting over cautious or anticipating problems and overflanking this will help a lot. Sometimes people will stop the dog and hope the sheep will drift through the gates; this may allow the sheep to stop or move past the gates. It may be better to keep your dog on his feet and moving without pushing too hard in order to put the sheep through the gates.

If your dog will not flank accurately or pushes too hard while flanking this may also cause you to miss gates. If you try to bring the sheep too close to one side of the panels they may split and some go through the gates and some go around. All of these are the result of nervousness on the part of the handler, flanking problems or inability to read the sheep.

Other problems that may occur at the drive gates include playing it 'too safe' and allowing the sheep to go too far past the panels before attempting to make the turn. This can seriously affect the cross drive. Some sheep will relax, change their head carriage or change the way they hold their ears when they pass through the panels; be observant and see if the sheep will 'tell' you when they are through the gates.

You will have the same types of problems with the second drive gate or cross-drive gate except that you are looking at and approaching this gate from a different angle. If you are an inexperienced handler it may be helpful to make a banana-shaped cross drive with the bow of the banana coming toward the handler so that you can turn the sheep's heads into the second drive gate as you see them come into the window of the panels of this obstacle. This will help you learn to see the drive gate and read the sheep on the cross drive. It will result in deduction of points since you have not moved the sheep in a straight line between the sets of gates. But, it may be worth taking the deduction in order to keep things under control and learn to hit the gates.

Practicing driving to gates is important. Change the angle of the gates, how they are positioned and how they are placed in the terrain. Sometimes gates will be set an angle, sometimes in a hollow, on a slope or close to a fence. All of these factors will influence how the sheep approach the gates and the way that you will have to read and handle the sheep in order to get them through them.

You will need to practice the course backwards to practice a pull through. A pull through is when you go around the back of the gate and bring the sheep through the opening coming towards you instead of away from you. Some courses or judges will require this variation. If you do not practice it you will not be familiar with what is required.

Pressures on the Cross Drive—Pressures on the dog and sheep will be different on the cross drive than when you are driving sheep away from the handler. There may be pressure to the set-out pen or to the exhaust pen that exert a pull on the sheep. The dog may have to be off to one side to hold this pressure and may be reluctant to let go of this pressure in order to flank when asked. If you have to do a correction on the cross drive, make sure that you go out to the dog's head and get in front of him. Don't come up behind the dog in order to correct him. You will have to walk out to make these corrections. If you constantly have to walk out to the dog on the cross drive to make a correction, go back to basics and work close at hand before attempting things at a distance and on the cross drive again.

Be aware that the pressure may change at some point as you go across the cross drive. You may have to make adjustments from one side of the sheep to the other, push at one place or have your dog release the pressure and push very little at another.

If there are landmarks (rocks, grass, flowers or dirt patches or different shades of grass) this may help you determine when the sheep are on-line during the cross drive. It is helpful to walk the course and to watch a friend walk the course in order to determine the line for the cross drive.

Setting Up for the Shed/Split or Pen—As you complete the last leg of the drive, you will need to be thinking about and planning how you will set up for the shed/split or pen. The judging of the next phase of work starts approximately 2/3 to 3/4 of the way down the last leg of the drive if going to the pen or when the sheep cross the line of the shedding ring in preparation for shedding.

It is important to remember to keep the sheep on-line for the last leg of the drive. The line should be from the edge of the cross-drive gates to the pen or the center of the shedding ring. It is easy to forget to keep the sheep on line and you can lose a lot of points for this!

If you are bringing the sheep to the pen, you should be trying to bring the sheep to the middle of the opening if the pen mouth is in line with the last leg of the drive. Sometimes the pen will be set so the sheep have to go down the side and turn to go into the mouth of the pen. The ideal pen would be for the sheep to walk right in, with a minimum of deviation, no circling of the pen and no turning back to face the dog. This rarely happens! The way that you bring them down the last leg of the drive in order to line them up, will influence the ease with which you pen. If the sheep are nervous and panic it will make penning very difficult!

If you are bringing the sheep to the shedding ring, it is helpful to have a plan for how you are going to shed. With some sheep it may be possible to line them up as you approach the shedding ring. Then you can shed as the sheep move past you in single file. Refer to the Chapter on Shedding and Splitting for more details on this approach. With other types of sheep it may be necessary to bring them into the shedding ring and let them settle in a group before trying to shed.

Concluding Remarks

Driving can be difficult for some dogs and many handlers. Practice, patience and persistence will pay off over time. Be sure to practice in as many places and situations as possible.

THE PEN

Introduction

The pen may follow the last leg of the drive or be after the shed. The sheep should be regrouped after the shed and move in a direct line to the pen. The pen may be followed by a single if a full international-style course is done or the course may be completed when the sheep have been penned. Some of the most common problems at the pen are the result of handler error and a lack of partnership with the dog at the pen.

When you first practice penning, be sure that you use tame sheep that can be penned relatively easily so he can have some success. This can help create the pattern for penning and help him learn the purpose of the job when you stand by the pen. If the dog does not flank, stop, out, back or obey other commands at the pen, forget about getting the sheep in the pen and make sure that the dog takes these commands correctly. Then come back and try to get the sheep in the pen again. Later you will need to practice penning with more challenging sheep.

Components of the Pen

The components or basic tools that you will need at the pen include:

1. Walk Up
2. Flanks
3. Back and/or Out
4. Stop
5. Hold/break back to cover
6. Teamwork between the handler and dog

1. Walk Up

Your dog will have to walk up to put the sheep into the pen. If you cannot get the dog to walk into pressure and release pressure you will have problems penning your sheep.

2. Flanks

The ability to flank your dog accurately and precisely will be important at the pen. Different types of flanks will be important at the pen—you will need to be able to flank your fast and slow, short and long, or in and out.

3. Stop

You will need to be able to stop your dog. Sometimes it may be better to stop your dog by lying him down in order to relieve pressure. At other times at the pen it may be better to stop the dog on his feet and have him hold pressure.

4. Back and/or Out

An OUT will be important to widen flanks or to move the dog laterally without forward motion. A BACK can be very handy to get the dog to release a little pressure on the sheep so that they do not move past you or so that he can step back and cover sheep that may want to break or go around the pen.

5. Hold Stock/Break Back to Cover

We have explained exercises in other chapters that helped your dog learn to hold stock and break back to cover his stock. This is extremely important at the pen. Often the dog will tend to come into his stock, particularly if they want to circle the pen. Sometimes he will want to grip in order to control the sheep. By learning to hold stock and break back to cover your dog will be less likely to do this and you will be more likely to be able to recover should you or the dog make a small mistake.

6. *Handler Doing His/Her Part*

All of the stock work requires teamwork on the part of the handler and dog. At the pen there is a fine line between the handler doing his/her share and taking the work away from the dog. In a trial situation the handler needs to help the dog, but not do the majority of the work of penning the sheep. The ideal situation would be for the dog to do all the work, but this is not always practical or possible, either in a working situation or at a trial.

Problems at the Pen

Handler Errors

Handler errors are a big problem at the pen. Each sheep is an individual and will react differently at the pen. You will need to work them so that you can get all the individuals to cooperate and move into the pen. One sheep may require very little pressure, while another will take a lot of pressure. You may have to move a sheep from the outside to the inside; learning to roll the sheep around will sometimes be helpful in getting sheep into the pen. Refer to the Chapter on Shedding and Splitting for more details on rolling sheep or shuffling sheep.

One problem that frequently occurs is that the handler will use the crook as a tool to help influence or move the dog, instead of using it as a tool to help influence or move the sheep. This may create unnecessary or unwanted movement of the sheep or keep the sheep from going into the pen. Don't come to rely on the crook or any training tool to the extent that you cannot move the dog without it. A training tool is a tool only and shouldn't be a substitute for verbal or whistle control or a response to body language.

Another problem is when the handler puts too much pressure on the sheep and drives them back towards the dog. Usually they will then try to go around the corner of the pen. You will want to be observant and learn to read the sheep. Learn to put pressure on the sheep that needs the pressure and not the sheep that do not need the pressure.

Another common problem is when the handler watches the dog instead of the sheep. In all parts of a trial or general sheepwork, the handler should be able to look at the whole picture and not focus on just one part. He/She should be aware of both the dog and sheep. Often the sheep will tell you where the dog is and where the dog needs to be. To learn to do this, you should practice watching the sheep when watching other people work. See if you can predict which sheep will be the first to move, which sheep will break or which sheep will lead the other sheep into the pen.

Another problem is when the handler does not hold his/her side of the sheep at the pen. If the dog is crowding the sheep it may be impossible, but there are many times when the handler needs to step up and block the sheep, use the crook to influence the sheep or use whatever body language it takes to move sheep into the pen. Make sure that the dog releases the pressure sufficiently on his side; if you push the sheep back onto the dog with too much pressure it may result in the sheep breaking or going around the pen or may encourage the dog to grip or come into the sheep.

The Dog That Grips at the Pen or Won't Fall Back and Cover

This is a relatively common problem in a high pressure situation at the pen. It may occur when the dog walks up very close to a sheep that will not move and he feels that he has no choice but to escalate the pressure to a grip. More commonly it occurs when a sheep breaks or runs around the side of the pen. The dog may be excited in this situation and fly in and grip in order to try to control the sheep. You will need to scold him for this and have him get OUT so that he covers the sheep to bring it back instead of coming onto the sheep.

The exercises described in the Chapters on Shedding and Splitting and Building Interest will help you and your dog learn about holding sheep and learning to step back and cover sheep in high pressure situations. Practicing these things will help!

Dog Won't Walk Up to Push the Sheep Into the Pen

Refer to the Chapter on Teaching the Walk Up for details on teaching the basics of walking up. If your dog will not walk up in the pen, go back to the basics.

Taking the Sheep Out of the Pen

After the pen has been completed, you will have to take the sheep out of the pen in order to exhaust them or to take them to the shedding ring. I like the dog to be beside me at the corner of the pen. As I start to open the gate, I will flank him in the direction that the gate opens. I like him to arrive at the back corner of the pen on the same side as the gate with sufficient distance to walk up and encourage the sheep to move out of the pen. I consider this to be an advantage because it will turn the sheep to move toward the opening of the gate, not toward the gate itself as it opens. It also keeps the dog in a position to cover both directions at the back of the pen should the sheep try to escape in this direction after exiting the pen. Also, it allows the handler and dog to stay on opposite sides of the sheep, without crossing the path of the sheep as they move into the shedding ring. The sheep should move in a direct line from the pen to the shedding ring. Some situations may require different positioning of the dog to deal with unique pressures, but this positioning provides a good rule of thumb for moving sheep out of the pen.

The dog should not anticipate and swing around to the back of the pen on his own. The dog should wait for you to ask him to flank to the back of the pen. You will be surprised how many dogs do this on their own initiative. If they have been asked to do it once they will often remember. If they do it too soon it may push the sheep right back out of the pen before you have the gate closed.

If your dog is correctly positioned at the back of the pen, he will be able to flank around and hold the sheep so that they can be moved to the exhaust pen or so that they can move to the shedding ring. If you are taking the sheep to the exhaust pen, be sure that you do this in an orderly manner. Do not be so relieved that your course is completed that you neglect to handle the sheep in a workmanlike way on the way to the exhaust pen. Take them on a direct line to the exhaust pen and do not overwork them on the way. This is good stockmanship and common courtesy. If a separate dog and handler are present to exhaust the sheep, honor the work of this dog and call your dog off. Put him on a leash if you need to. This is not a time to train your dog!

Exercises for Penning

There are several types of pens or obstacles that can be set up in order to practice penning. One that you can use to increase your expertise at penning is made with 3 panels. Two of the panels are set to make a V. The third panel is attached to one leg of the V to make a wing at a 45 degree angle on the V (Diagram 7). You will want to stand at the end of the wing on the V. You cannot move the wing; it stays stable. You will want to pen the sheep in the V. This will require inching them into the pen. If you push them too hard or too far they will easily come out of the V. This will help you learn how to move your dog at the pen.

Another interesting obstacle is a Maltese cross. This takes 8 panels, each set up in an L to create two intersecting chutes at right angles to each other (Diagram 8). You will have to put the sheep through one chute, then turn them and bring them around to go through the chute that is at right angles. The handler can move in the area to one side of the chutes. The Maltese cross will help you learn how to hold your side at the pen and how to move to help influence the sheep to go into a narrow space. If you are having trouble with this at first, move the chute so it is wider. Eventually you should be able to do a Maltese cross that has openings of the chutes that are barely the width of a sheep.

Diagram 7

V-Panel Exercise for Penning

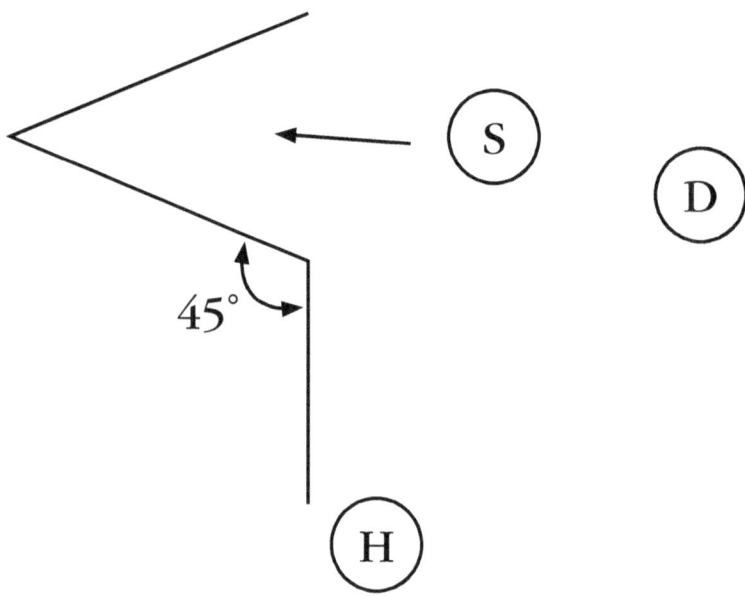

A v-shaped "pen" is made with 2 panels and a wing made at an approximately 45° angle. It will require precise control to put sheep into the v-shaped pen.

Diagram 8

The Maltese Cross

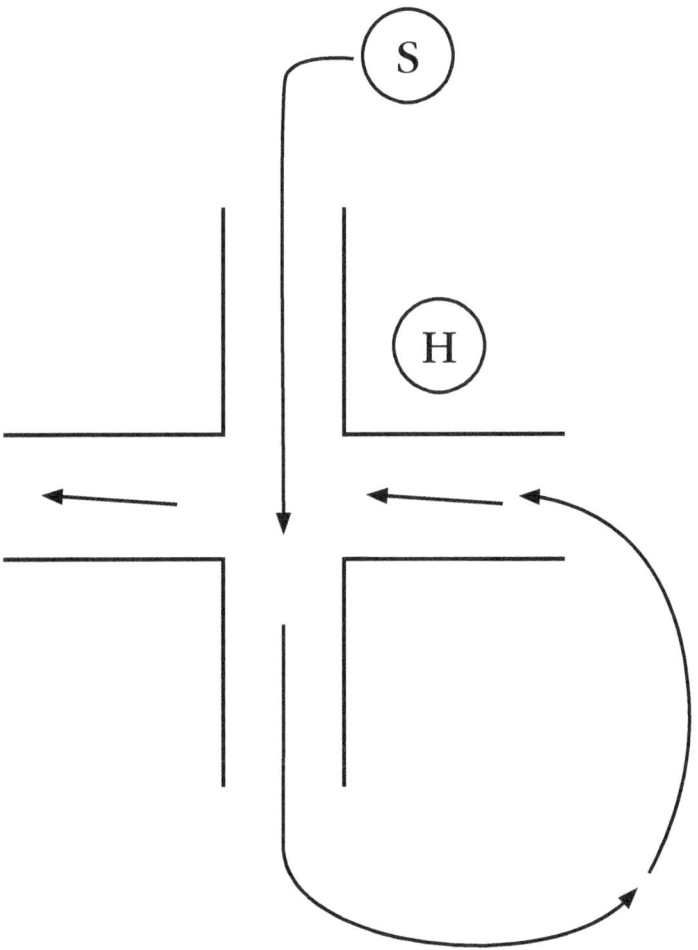

This shows the path of the sheep navigating the Maltese cross. The handler stays within the quadrant indicated while the dog is moved to guide the sheep. This can be done from any quadrant of the Maltese cross with adjustments in the path to make the same pattern.

Concluding Remarks

Developing your skills at penning and your dog's skills at penning will take time and patience. Practice penning at a variety of places and with various types of sheep. Be sure that you set up the pen in a variety of places.

Some handlers will not set up a pen at home. I feel it is an advantage to practice this and familiarize yourself and your dog with the job at hand.

Mick, the Kelpie, working longhorns

SHED AND SPLIT

Introduction

Shedding or splitting stock is a practical exercise that most anyone will use if they keep more than a few head of any kind of stock. Splitting stock refers to separation of one or more head of stock from a group; this may be done in order to move selected individuals such as removal of rams after the breeding season, separation of ill or injured individuals for observation, treatment or confinement or separation of individuals to be sold or transported. A split may specify the number of sheep which should be separated from a group, but often does not specify the manner in which this is accomplished. Shedding refers to a particular type of separation of stock; in this situation one or two sheep are separated from a larger group and held apart. When a single sheep is separated from the group this is often referred to as a single. There may be a shed of two sheep from the group prior to the pen, followed by a single at international style ISDS, USBCHA, AKC or AHBA competitions.

The sheep to be separated are usually designated verbally (as in back two sheep or back sheep, referring to the position of the sheep to be separated relative to others in the group). The manner in which the shed should be conducted is usually specified (as in 'on the nose', meaning with the sheep facing the dog; or on the nose in order to receive full points—this indicates that positions other than this will not receive full points). An international shed refers to separation of specifically marked or designated sheep from a group by allowing the escape of the non-designated sheep from the larger group. The dog should be used to prevent the movement of marked stock to join the unmarked, separated stock. The handler is instrumental in setting up the opportunity for unmarked stock to separate from the marked or designated stock.

Many dogs enjoy this type of job, but it is important to establish a firm foundation before teaching this job since some dogs may have a tendency to leave individuals or separate individuals spontaneously if taught to shed too early or without a proper foundation. Experienced trainers may be able to incorporate many elementary exercises applicable to shedding and splitting when they see opportunities arise during training or working sessions. However, if this is your first experience with shedding/splitting, make sure that you have thoroughly mastered the exercises in previous chapters.

Competition Application

Shedding stock is an advanced exercise that is included in the highest levels of competitions of most herding organizations. Occasionally a shed or split will be called for at an intermediate level, but the degree of sophistication and expectations will usually be less than that required at the highest levels of competition. As a competition exercise, the purpose of the shed is to show that the dog will come into the sheep and hold one or several sheep away from the others and demonstrate control of this/these sheep. It is a test of the dog's obedience and a test of power since a weak dog may not be able to effectively hold one or several determined sheep away from the others. However, in some situations, we may be asking even the most powerful, obedient and experienced dog to accomplish the impossible!

Although most competition rules will specifically state that the dog should accomplish the shed (not the handler), it is truly an act of teamwork. The most accomplished handlers will be helping their dogs or upholding their side of the task in a way that makes it appear that the dog is doing it on his own or with little help from the handler!

Only by observation of accomplished handlers will you be able to observe expert shedding. The standard of shedding varies tremendously in regional competitions and judges may fail to penalize competitors for substandard performance. Even with extremely difficult stock, the judge should leave room to reward the dog and handler lucky enough and/or accomplished enough to perform in the ideal manner.

At advanced levels of competition it is sometimes said to become a penning and shedding contest. This recognizes the fact that many top competitors may be able to have a high-scoring run that is separated by the final tasks of penning or shedding.

Components of the Shed

Experienced handlers may not be aware of the body language they use, the way they signal their dog and the ways that they put pressure on sheep. Experienced handlers may rely on their superior ability to read stock and feel the situation in order to accomplish the desired goal. But, for the less experienced, it may be useful to view the shed as a composite of a number of components, some of which can be addressed singly and which may eventually be synthesized to create the final goal.

Some of the exercises that we have previously introduced are of benefit in teaching the shed/split and you should review these exercises in previous chapters. Exercises to review and to address some aspects of these components will be covered later in this chapter. Components of the shed include:

1. Handler refining the ability to read the sheep.
2. Dog able to hold sheep without advancing or creating unnecessary movement of the stock. This should include the ability of the dog to withstand the pressure of sheep being pushed onto him (see below) and to withstand movement of the handler while manipulating the sheep without advancing on the

stock or creating havoc. It is an important part of getting the stock to settle and in setting the stage for a successful shed.

3. Ability of the handler to hold his/her side of the stock. This is an important part of the shed and may be a new concept for inexperienced handlers who have previously moved away with sheep, put sheep in a pen or relied on a fence to hold stock in a particular area once the dog has brought them to you.

4. Ability of the handler to manipulate the stock. This may include the ability to turn the head of the stock or to shuffle individuals to particular positions in relation to other individuals within the group in preparation for the separation of the desired individual(s). This will include work by the handler alone and in combination with the dog to position the sheep in a way that will enable the shed to be accomplished.

5. Ability of the dog to advance on the stock or give ground and hold, when requested to do so. We have previously defined a need for the dog to hold sheep without advancing on them (see number 2 above). But, if asked, the dog should be able to advance on the stock and come to within a distance of the stock that will enable the dog to come into or through the stock in order to create and maintain their separation. If the dog is too far away or will not advance on the stock, it doesn't matter how fast he comes through, he may not be fast enough to achieve a position that will enable him to control the stock. It is a combination of positioning, speed, distance from the stock and the reaction of the stock that comes into play in determining the final accomplishment of the shed. It is a common misconception of inexperienced handlers that speed is the answer to shedding. It may certainly be a useful characteristic to have in many situations, but is only one of many factors that comes into play!

6. An obedient dog that will promptly come through the sheep when asked to do so. This is not simply a recall or calling the dog off. That is why I recommend that a specific command be given for this action that is not the same as any other command

for the dog. It should mean a specific job to the dog. In combination with your body language it will come to mean a specific task that should be accomplished in a particular way!

7. Ability of the dog to hold the separated sheep and demonstrate control of those sheep. This is what most people think of as the shed, although there are a number of components that we've listed that lead up this final culmination. The dog should not run after, chase or grip the sheep to be held, but demonstrate quiet control over the separated sheep with the ability to move these sheep off, if and when directed to do so by the handler. Some dogs may have trouble concentrating on the sheep that have been separated and worry about the other sheep that have gotten away, while other dogs may be so focused on the sheep that have been separated that they loose the BIG PICTURE and may become so focused on the separated sheep that it may be difficult to break their concentration or to get movement in the direction or manner that is desired.

8. Performance of the LOOK BACK to regroup sheep, if needed. If a shed is performed before the pen or the sheep need to be regrouped during practical work or exhausted following successful completion of a single, then the dog should be able to regroup the sheep and proceed to the pen or proceed to the next phase of work. This may be more difficult than it would first appear since the dog is now being asked to undo what we've just had him do, may be excited by the shed or single, or may be disoriented with regard to the position of the sheep to be regrouped.

It may be useful to have a specific word or command for shedding or splitting stock. Some people will use 'that'll do' or 'here', but I find that a separate command helps the dog learn the job and keep his concentration on the stock.

Another important aspect is the posture or positioning that you adopt as a signal to your dog that the job at hand is the shed or single. When holding the sheep and spreading them out to position them for the shed, you may be squarely facing the sheep and dog, or slightly angled to funnel them past you in single file. The amount of pressure that you will have to apply and the posture and positioning of your body will depend on the reaction of the sheep and how easily they are influenced to move. When you are ready to have the dog come in, you will be turning sideways to face the nose(s) of the sheep to be separated and held, you are signaling to your dog that these are the sheep that you want. This may be a very quick and/or subtle change in body position. If the sheep are very light, you may adopt this position earlier in the procedure in order to subtly influence the sheep and dog. As the sheep change direction or are manipulated to set up the shed, you will have to change your position so that you maintain this orientation (facing the noses of the sheep that you want to separate). You will see too many handlers that face their dog squarely across the sheep when asking their dog to come in—often with disastrous results—the dog may not come in or may focus on the wrong group of sheep!

This will take a lot of practice in order to get your timing, posture, pressure and dog and sheep positioning coordinated. Things can change rapidly when you are working with sheep in an open area. That is why many of the exercises for this chapter emphasize using sheep in a small area in which the components can be broken down into steps that can be more easily controlled for the novice dog and handler a little at a time.

When you are about to ask your dog to come in, you may want to make a slight movement across the face of the sheep in order to create a moment of hesitation that will allow your dog to come in. In some cases there will be only a fleeting moment within which your dog will have to respond in order to successfully complete the shed. As the dog comes in, step backwards, with your crook behind you. This will discourage the sheep from breaking back behind you. The distance that you must move backwards and how rapidly you move back will depend on the sheep and their response. The most important thing is not to stand rock still and allow the sheep to close back in around you! This is a common mistake with novice handlers and will even catch out some experienced handlers at times. As you back out of the way, be sure to turn toward the group of sheep that you have shed off. You may move slightly toward the heads of these sheep as you move. Do not turn the dog towards the tails of the sheep that are moving away.

Teaching and Learning Various Components of the Shed/Split

1. Learning to read stock

Previous chapters have emphasized situations in which you can increase your ability to read stock.

The goal is to set up a controlled situation in which the stock are moving or can be moved relatively slowly so that you can note subtle changes that signal the intention to move and note the degree of pressure that is need in order to produce movement of a given magnitude.

Exercise 1: Observation

Observation of sheep with and without pressure from handler and dog. Put a group of sheep on the fence, take the time let the sheep settle and observe them without pressure, noting the positions they take and the amount of tension visible in their body language. Then apply pressure by moving back and forth or around the stock, noting which sheep move, when they move relative to your movement and subtle features that suggest they are thinking about moving (such as raising of the head or change in position of the ears or turning of the head or unnatural tension because of pressure). This will teach you about your body pressure and its effect on the stock.

Then move your dog in short flanks and walk up to the sheep, without creating movement or only slight movement of the stock. Be a keen observer of the effects the pressure of the dog has on each individual within the group. Chances are it will be different than the features you observed in response to your body language alone!

Exercise 2: Movement

Movement of specific sheep. Then see if, by a combination of your movement and movement of the dog, you can get a specific sheep within the group to move. Remember, only slight movement is what you are after in this stage. The individual doesn't have to move far or fast. See if you can get a slight turn of the head or slight change in position. Pick the individual that you would like to move. Don't worry too much about movement of other sheep, but movement by the other sheep should be limited.

Exercise 3: Shuffling

Shuffling sheep. This exercise is still done on the fence with a group of relatively tame sheep. Now that you have the ability to move a particular sheep, pick a sheep on the outside and see if you can roll it around the other sheep in order to get it to the other side. There should be little movement of the other sheep. If you have a group that exceeds 5 sheep, the dog will likely have to move the sheep to the other side and may need to move with the sheep in order to accomplish this.

2. Dog able to hold stock without advancing or creating movement.

Exercise 1: Holding

Holding sheep. In previous chapters we have described this as one of the basics during early training. Briefly, to review, your dog should be able to tuck sheep in behind you when you stop a short distance from a fence. He should be able to hold sheep in front of you at your feet when you stop directly on a fence or in the open. He should be able to step back and cover sheep and hold them to you if you put pressure on the sheep that moves the sheep toward the dog or if a sheep tries to escape to one side or the other.

He should be able to do this with the handler positioned between the dog and the sheep, when sheep are between the dog and the handler or when the dog is between the handler and the sheep.

Exercise 2: Back

Back. This is another part of the basic foundation work that has been covered previously. This command may be very useful in a variety of situations, including the shed. It can be used to help relieve and then reapply pressure or to help position the dog to hold or settle the sheep. Remember that the dog should move away from the stock without turning away from the stock.

3. and 4. Handler should be able to hold their side of the stock and manipulate stock.

In addition to the exercises for reading stock(see above), there are several other exercises that are useful for helping the handler learn to manipulate stock.

Exercise 1: Move Stock Without Dog

Handler moves stock without dog. The handler should be able to move stock and hold them in an area without the aid of a dog. This should include moving in a small area to begin with, as well as in open spaces. The ease with which this can be accomplished will depend, to a large extent, on whether the sheep are used to being handled and how heavy or light they are. Experience with stock of various types is very useful since some breeds or types of sheep may respond differently to the handler's body language. The movement of the stock is of less importance than you learning to read the response of the sheep to your pressure.

Exercise 2: Pushing Sheep

Handler pushing sheep to the dog. For this exercise, have the dog bring the sheep to your feet. Ideally the dog should be on his feet, holding the sheep to you. At first it may be necessary to have the dog lie down in order to understand this exercise. The handler should exert pressure on the sheep to move them toward the dog and to cause the sheep to spread out between the dog and the handler. It may take a bit of trial-and-error to determine the correct distance between the sheep and the dog to allow this type of movement. The distance between the sheep and the dog may have to be greater in the initial learning stages of this exercise compared to more advanced work when the dog will be able to be closer and accept this kind of pressure.

Things that may go wrong with this exercise include:

- Sheep splitting and running away. In order to prevent this, try it first in a smaller area and with only a little pressure on the sheep. Do not rush this in order to have the sheep stay settled.
- Sheep run over the top of the dog. Be sensitive to the amount of pressure that you are putting on the sheep. You do not want to push the sheep over or around the dog, just toward him! Likewise, you do not want the dog to exert pressure that will push the sheep over or behind you. You may have to ask the dog to come in and exert a little more pressure on the sheep, or you may have to ask him to step back (Back) and take a bit of the pressure off.
- Dog explodes into the sheep or chases sheep. It may be that you have proceeded too rapidly with this exercise or that the dog is uncomfortable with the pressure exerted by you and/or the sheep. This can be very uncomfortable for the dog during the early stages since he is used to sheep moving AWAY from him, not toward him and may consider this a threat or a situation that needs some force. You will have to be able to stop your dog and may have to ask him to lie down or back off if he wants to advance on the sheep as they move toward him, if he wants to explode into the sheep or if he wants to chase them.

Exercise 3: Stringing Sheep

Stringing sheep out in line between you and the dog while the sheep are moving.

There are 2 variations of this exercise. The first variation is driving the sheep in a line. Instead of having the sheep in a bunch, spread the sheep out so they are in a line, one behind the other and try to drive them across the field, maintaining this positioning. This will require the dog to hold his side of the sheep and the handler to hold his/her side of the sheep. Handler and/or dog may have to move back and forth in order to keep the pressure such that the line up of sheep is maintained. You should find that holes or openings between the sheep and which are appropriate for shedding magically appear when you try this exercise. This is a test of the ability of the dog and handler each to hold their side of the sheep.

The second variation is to learn to have the sheep come toward and past you in a line. You will want to position the dog and sheep so they are coming toward you, as they would on the last leg of the drive. Flank the dog with small movements to the side and back of the sheep in order to have them walking toward you in a line, one behind the other. This is in preparation for setting up the shed and a more advanced exercise in shedding whereby the dog will come through the sheep as they are moving past you. To begin with, try to have the sheep move past you in single file. When you can accomplish this, you are then ready to try it with a shed. As the sheep are moving past you, you will likely need to flank your dog slightly in front of the last sheep's eye and then have him come in to hold the single sheep to you.

You may then want to have the dog wear (fetch) the single sheep to you as you move around the field. You will want to use a relatively tame sheep for this at the start since working a single is hard for many dogs at first. This exercise may take many tries before you develop your timing in flanking the dog and having the dog in the correct place to accomplish this task. Be patient and work at this over time. Don't overdo this by attempting this repeatedly within a single training session; once or twice per training session will likely be plenty.

5. *Ability of the dog to advance on the stock or give ground and hold, when requested to do so.*

In order to shed or single, the dog will have to advance on the stock or give ground and hold. Some aspects of this have been covered in previous chapters on foundation basics, but specific exercises that are helpful with shedding also apply.

Exercise 1: Walking

Dog learning to walk into sheep with pressure and release. The objective of this exercise is to teach the dog to walk up to the sheep and be comfortable holding pressure. Again, starting with tame sheep in a contained area is required. Start with you dog on a leash or line.

Have the sheep on the fence. You will have the dog on leash at your side. Have the dog walk up onto the sheep. He should walk slowly and steadily. You will walk with him initially, encouraging him if he becomes unsure of himself or steadying him if he wants to rush, grip or move too rapidly. You may want to walk up a short ways and then stand, allowing the dog and sheep to settle. This is a good place to practice the BACK. Be sure that you do not BACK every time you stop him. By asking him to BACK and then walk up again you will be helping him to learn to exert and release pressure. Depending on the reaction of the sheep and the dog, you may be able to walk right up to the sheep. It does not matter if he is walking up to the nose, tail or side of the sheep. As long as your dog will walk up when asked, stand when asked, and remain calm, this fulfills the objective of this exercise. You should be able to do this on leash and by the dog's side at first. Then you should be able to have the dog do this dragging the leash and then without the leash, while you are standing in a variety of positions relative to the sheep and the dog.

Exercise 2: Shedding on the Fence

Once you can comfortably accomplish Exercise 1 (see above), you are ready to try shedding on the fence. There are several variations of this exercise based on the position of the handler relative to the sheep and the dog. At first you will do as you have done for Exercise 1 and have your dog on a leash and by your side. Walk your dog up to the sheep and then between them, making a hole yourself, if necessary. As you walk between the sheep, turn so that the dog is facing one group of sheep. It is helpful if you are on the inside (toward the center of the enclosure) with the dog between you and the fence. Remember that the dog has to walk into the face of the sheep in order to push the one back that you want to keep. It is important that at this point you always have the dog come in so that he is turning to face the sheep's face. That way he will learn that this is the positioning of the sheep that you want him to hold. This will teach him to shed sheep on the nose. It may be difficult to teach if the sheep are skittish and turn quickly away from the dog. If the sheep are skittish, you may have to resort to tying a single sheep by a collar in order to keep it in a position that will allow control of the situation. Training sheep to tie by a collar and some examples of when this may be helpful has been covered in the section on Teaching the Sheep to Tie. It is helpful to use the word you have chosen to indicate the shed or single to your dog (I use 'cut') as you come between the sheep and turn to face the single sheep to be held. At this point you will not worry about taking the single anywhere (particularly if using a tied sheep). The dog should turn and stand quietly, facing the sheep.

The next phase of this exercise is to have the dog off leash and do the same thing. You will likely still be by his side, but will not have a leash. As he comes in and turns to face the single sheep, you will move to the far side of the sheep, as you would for him to fetch the sheep to you. If the sheep is free (not tied), you may do a small amount of wearing of this sheep with the dog holding it to you.

Once comfortable in this position, you can position yourself on the fence with the sheep between you and the dog. You will flank the dog from side to side in order to spread the sheep out along the fence. With very heavy or dog-broke sheep, this may be difficult; the sheep may tend to face you and bury their heads at your knees or may turn and face the dog. In that case you will have the opportunity to teach him to walk into some very small spaces between the sheep! Access to heavier and lighter stock is necessary to train all parts of this exercise!

When he comes in between the sheep, turn him toward the heads of one group of sheep. At this time do not try to move the sheep, but just have the dog come in, turn toward the heads of the sheep to be held and stand quietly.

Also practice this exercise when you are positioned at either end of the group of sheep (not just straight across from the dog) or when the dog is between you and the sheep. Regardless of your position relative to the sheep or the dog, the dog should be able to walk in and turn to hold one or more sheep in a controlled situation. Once you've mastered this in a small area, try it in the open and with the sheep in the center of the field rather than on the fence. This can be a very challenging exercise and require extreme patience and good control.

DON'T OVERDO THIS, but practice it a few times over a number of training sessions.

6. *Obedient dog that will promptly come through the sheep when asked to do so.*

Up until this phase of training we have discouraged or reprimanded the dog when it has come into the middle of the sheep or come through and split the sheep. Now we need to be sure that the dog is comfortable coming into and through stock when asked to do so.

You will have already had your dog comfortable walking up to the sheep and through the sheep as described above and covered in foundation training. Your dog should come readily to you when recalled, on and off the sheep. You should already have introduced the command for shedding/splitting that you have chosen to use. If this foundation work has been done there should be few problems with the dog coming in rapidly enough. But, if your dog is reluctant to come in, does not come in when asked to do so or comes in slowly, there are some things that you can do.

- You can put your dog on a leash in a small area containing sheep. Then walk through the sheep, sometimes stopping and standing in the midst of the sheep, then continuing on walking through, around and by the sheep. Repeat this until the dog becomes comfortable on leash. Then do this without the leash. The dog should be by your side (not in front of you or behind you). You may want to teach your dog a command for positioning himself by your right and left side (separate commands for each side). Be sure that your dog is equally comfortable on either side of you. Just like with flanks, it is likely that you and/or your dog will be more comfortable on one side than the other to start with.
- Start out with the dog walking by your side. Then have him stop and stand, while you continue walking through the sheep. Then turn and ask the dog to come into the sheep. Be sure to use the body positioning described in the Introduction to this chapter so that you indicate to the dog the sheep that you want

him to turn onto. If the dog is focused on the rest of the sheep and won't come through to the group that you want, forget about the sheep and call the dog to your feet, as if you are doing a split. At that moment the sheep do not matter; having the dog come to you is all that is important at this stage. If the dog will not come to you, you will not be able to accomplish the shed!

- If your dog is slow to come in, but is proficient at other parts of the shed, you may increase his enthusiasm by doing the following:

Have the dog drive one group of sheep away from you. Have a second group of sheep behind you some distance away. Then have the dog flank around the sheep and bring them back toward you. Try not to have them moving too fast at this point, but you will want to have them moving somewhat briskly back toward the second group of sheep. Then flank the dog around to one side of the sheep and call him in to stop the sheep from reaching the other group.

Usually the movement of the sheep and the dog's desire to control the sheep will help ensure that he comes in rapidly. The SPACING between the groups of sheep and the TIMING of the call-in are important for this exercise to work. Leave enough room between the sheep so that the dog will have time to come into position to stop the returning group of sheep and will not be confused and try to go around both groups of sheep.

7. *Ability of the dog to hold the separated sheep and demonstrate control of those sheep.*

This is an important part of the shed/single. To satisfy discerning judges and receive maximum points for the shed, the dog must demonstrate control of the separated sheep. This usually involves moving the sheep a distance away by driving.

8. Performance of the LOOK BACK to regroup sheep, if needed

After the sheep have been shed and the dog has demonstrated control of the sheep, you may need to regroup the sheep. This is where the LOOK BACK will be used. Teaching the LOOK BACK has been covered in the Chapter on Teaching the Look Back. Problems that frequently occur with the LOOK BACK following the shed/single are:

- Dog is so focused on the sheep that he is controlling that he does not take the LOOK BACK for the other group of sheep. In order to break his concentration on the sheep that he is controlling, stop the dog. Walk out to him and toward the group of sheep that you want him to LOOK BACK for. Do NOT look at or focus on the sheep that he was controlling. Look at the sheep you now want him to get.

    If you have to, call the dog to you and walk toward the group of sheep until he focuses on them. Then send him on a flank around them.

    Make sure that you practice the LOOK BACK with flanks in both directions.

- Dog goes straight back into the sheep or chases the sheep. Once the dog takes the LOOK BACK, stop him. Then position yourself between the dog and the group of sheep before flanking him around these sheep. This way you are in a position to make sure that he flanks squarely and wide enough to get around his sheep without going through the middle of them or turning it into a chase. Once the dog has flanked around the sheep, stop him so that he does not chase the sheep back toward the other group. Then flank him around the entire group as they rejoin.

Concluding Remarks

The shed or single is a complicated task because there are so many parts to it. Many people practice the same mistakes with the shed/single over and over again. If you take your time, making sure that you and your dog are proficient at each component and exercise, you will be more likely to develop good shedding/singling skills. Don't get stuck on practicing a single piece of this that may not be to your liking. Practice many pieces of this task in order to improve the whole picture! Watching a well-executed shed or single can look incredibly simple. Only those that have truly studied it can appreciate the complexity of this task.

It is hard to do a shed without the dog understanding the task you want him to do. The dog will have to have interest, flank left and right, stop, put pressure on and take pressure off, come into you and a look back. This encompasses 7 of the 8 basic tools for working sheep!

So, if you are having a problem with shedding, go back to the basics and work on the problem at the foundation level to help the shed/single. Do not work on the shed/single itself, but work on the basic tools for herding in order to solve the problem. Then come back to the shed or single.

INTRODUCTION TO WORKING DUCKS AND CATTLE

Introduction

Working ducks or cattle, particularly for trial competitions, can be developed to a high level of sophistication and detail. This chapter will not deal with advanced training or trialing on ducks or cattle, but will present some aspects of working ducks that will be important for those who do not have experience with this type of livestock or who are just starting to work their dog on ducks or cattle.

Up to this point, this book has dealt with starting dogs and teaching them the basic commands on sheep. This is my preference since the dog and sheep are less likely to get hurt. Cattle have a tendency to pull the dog in since he will come in tighter and try to exert pressure. Ducks may encourage the prey instinct in young dogs, but are very helpful for puppies or for people who may have limited access to other types of livestock or do not have much space. If you have trouble controlling your dog it will be better to start him on sheep. Ducks have very fragile bones and can easily be hurt by an overly enthusiastic or aggressive dog. Owning and caring for ducks may be a good introduction for people who have not previously owned stock.

Working Ducks

There are many different types of ducks. Some ducks are free moving, while others are heavy. Muscovy ducks may be difficult to work since they often freeze and don't flock together well. My favorite ducks are buff Indian Runner ducks or Indian Runner-Khaki-Campbel crosses. All varieties of ducks will work. Your choice of ducks will depend also on what you like and what you want to have around.

To start working ducks, you will need an enclosure. I prefer an approximately 20' x 40' enclosure, but it can be almost any size. It needs to be duck proof so that they cannot get out. You will likely need a training aid (rake, crook, bag, or other tool) and a rope. Once you can work your dog in a small area on ducks, it is important to be able to move to a larger area. This will help the dog learn to work at a greater distance from the stock and to widen out as he works. If you always stay in a small area, the dog may develop a habit of working too tight and too close to his stock. Sometimes when you take ducks out into the open you may lose a duck. Be prepared for the fact that you may not be able to find or recover this duck because he may run off and disappear or hide.

The reaction time of ducks is very quick. Ducks are good to use when trying to learn about reading livestock. Where-ever the head and beak is pointing is where they will go. If you put too much pressure on them, they may rotate their heads from side to side and/or start quacking. Just moving the ducks around yourself will help you learn to move livestock.

Ducks are good to start young puppies because they cannot outrun a puppy like a sheep sometimes can. They are not likely to run up and butt or jump on your puppy as some sheep will. They are good for developing interest in young puppies and I use ducks a lot for this. Be sure that the ducks you use for young puppies have been worked by experienced dogs. They need to have been worked in the center of the enclosure and not down the fence; this way they will go to the center of the enclosure and leave room for the dog to get around them. These ducks have been taught to come off the fence and to fetch toward the handler with work by more experienced dogs. If ducks lie down or will stand and stick their head through the fence; they are not accustomed to being worked by dogs. If you have ducks that do not want to cooperate and work, get rid of them. It is better to find some ducks that will help you and your dog. I prefer to have all drakes (males). Hens are always wanting to lay eggs and carry additional weight because of this. They may be carrying multiple eggs and it is not fair to ask them to work except for very short periods of time.

You will have to learn how to take care of and feed your ducks if you are going to work them. Too little or too much food will be detrimental. Talk to the experts at a hatchery who will be able to provide you with information about how to care for your ducks.

It is important to teach your dog to move ducks at the speed at which the ducks are comfortable, not the speed that would be appropriate for sheep. Ducks have short legs and should not be pushed too fast. If you constantly push ducks with too much pressure, they quickly will become difficult to work and you will have problems with them. Some people will repeatedly stop their dog in order to keep him from over-running the ducks. I prefer to teach the dog to pace himself and stay behind the ducks without repeated stopping. The exercises described for teaching the dog to release pressure and to step back and cover, as described in other chapters of this book, are good for teaching the dog to pace himself on ducks.

You can teach your dog all the commands on ducks, just as you would on sheep. Later in your training, ducks may be useful to put some polish on your dogs. The dog will have to learn to make quick, smooth and short movements instead of jerky or long movements in order move them smoothly. Ducks will not run to the handler so faults on the fetch may be more obvious. They are helpful in teaching the dog to pace himself and stay in the pocket. If a dog jumps out of the pocket on ducks, you will see it very quickly. Ducks will also help you determine whether you have an accurate stop on your dog because you are much closer to the dog than you would be on other types of stock. This is also helpful in giving a correction to enforce any element of your training. Some ducks may learn to run out and bite a dog. In this case the dog should be allowed to nip the duck in order to enforce his authority.

Ducks are also good for teaching the dog to back off of pressure and to step back and cover. The dog can see you over the top of the ducks and your position is closer to the stock than it would be with sheep. Therefore, you are in a better position to apply pressure or to correct your dog should he not give to the pressure appropriately.

Working Cattle

When starting to work cattle, you will need to remember that you are working an animal that is much larger than your dog. Remember to consider the safety of the dog and the cattle. Some people with a dog who grips and bites will put the dog on cattle and hope that the cattle will kick the dog and break him from gripping. This may help on cattle, but will not cure the problem when the dog is on sheep. The dog is smart enough to know the difference! I do not think it is worth taking the chance of getting your dog hurt by purposely putting him in this type of situation.

When I start a dog on cattle, I like to have a good level of control. The first thing I will teach him is to flank off cattle and not to draw into the cattle. This is because cattle tend to draw the dog into them. I want the dog to flank out far enough so that the cow can see the dog as he is moving, rather than running up under the cow's nose where he can get run over and hurt. I want my dog to flank out far enough out so that the cow can see him. This gives the cow the opportunity to react to the dog. This should make good sense since I do not appreciate being run over by cows and neither does the dog!

I prefer to use 3-5 yearling cattle of approximately 500-800 pounds for working dogs. I will want to start in an enclosure that is approximately 40' x 50' or someplace within which they cannot run fast or jump over fences. I do not like to start young dogs on smaller calves because he may tend to work only the calf when faced with a cow and calf because the calf presents less pressure than the cow and is easier to move. If a dog learns to work only the calf and is faced with a cow and calf, he may want to bite the calf in order to get it moving.

The calf will bawl and every cow in the pasture may then come after the dog to protect the calf! The cows learn not to trust the dog around their calves. By working cow and calves together after the dog has gained some experience, he will be less likely to cause problems.

Different breeds and categories of cattle respond to pressure in different ways. Heifers are usually easier to work because they move more freely than steers. Steers may be lazy, but will usually move along. Bulls can be quite pushy and will push back and will not always move where you want them to. In a group of cattle, you will have some that want to move, others that want to hold back and some that will go along with the pack. There are some types of cattle that are almost impossible to work!

Yearling cattle are usually very curious. When yearling cattle are first introduced to a dog, I like my dog to stand still and let the cattle come out to sniff him. When they reach out to sniff, I will want him to nip the nose. When they move off the dog, I will then ask the dog to walk up. I will let the cattle move off down the fence. When they go a short distance, I will flank the dog to the heads, making sure that he is back far enough for the cattle to see him when he arrives. Then I will have him stop and then walk up to bring them back. I will then gradually increase the distance that I move the cattle. Then I will move to a larger area and do the same type of work. In the larger area I will introduce some outruns and allow him to fetch them to a gate and put them through or to move them a short distance toward me.

I like to get this type of experience on a young dog before I take him to older cattle. Older cattle can be much more challenging. By having some experience on yearling calves, the dog is more likely to be able to handle older cattle. If working cows with calves, the dog may have to give ground repeatedly, but, at the same time, hold the pressure. When the cow stops and turns back to the calf, wait a bit and then have the dog walk back up and put pressure on the cow again. Even if the cow runs at the dog several times, if he will give ground but hold pressure and keep coming back and exerting pressure, the cow will learn that it is easier to get the calf up and move off with it than it is to stay and fight the dog. You need to allow the cow and calf to move off in the direction you want without crowding them. Calves can be very curious. If the calf comes back to sniff the dog, the cow may become very protective and also come back at the dog. If the dog crowds the cow and calf, the cow may decide to fight and you will never win the battle!

When working older cattle, I prefer to have two older, well schooled dogs that have experience with 500-800 pound cattle. I do not recommend working a young, inexperienced dog with an older, well schooled dog since he may create situations that will get BOTH dogs hurt. I am very careful since it only takes a blink of an eye for a 1,000 pound cow to seriously hurt a dog or damage his confidence to the point that he will not want to continue to work cattle.

I feel that a dog with bite is important for working cattle, but not as important as the ability to hold the pressure. If the dog will hold the pressure he will often not have to bite in order to get the cattle to move. If a dog is confident on cattle, he can make it look easy!

A dog that bites without thought, creates no thought. A dog that bites with thought, creates thought. This means that a dog should think about where, how and when to bite before he does it. This will result in a dog that learns to use good judgment about when a bite is needed and when it is not. A proper bite is on the nose, not on the side of the face or other places on the head. Heeling (biting low on the hind leg) is useful when moving cattle. Sometimes you do not want the dog to go to the head and you just want to have the dog make a cow move a little faster. This will require him to heel. Some dogs will not naturally heel, but will become better at this with practice. Heeling also requires judgment about which leg to bite and when. If the dog bites a leg as it comes off the ground, he will get kicked. He should bite the leg as weight is transferred onto it; that way he will not get kicked. I prefer a dog that will heel low, not high up on the hocks and I do not want to see a dog bite and swing on the tail of the cow.

Concluding Remarks

The opportunity to work a variety of types of stock is beneficial in helping you learn to read stock and in providing your dog with a balanced education.

Not all dogs are capable of working all types of livestock. It is the rare dog that will work all types of stock with equal ability and skill. But, you can teach many dogs to work some types of cattle, sheep or ducks.

If you do not have experience working a particular type of livestock, find someone who is experienced and knowledgeable to help you learn about reading the livestock and to introduce your dog to them.

Bob and Lynn

COMMON MYTHS AND MISCONCEPTIONS ABOUT HERDING

Introduction

There are many myths and misconceptions that you will hear about herding, herding dogs and training. I'm not sure why some of these have been perpetuated over the years, but the common myths and misconceptions continue to be propagated. They all have a little bit of truth in the correct situation, but many times the situation in which people are trying to apply them is not the correct one. Or, people may use these an excuse or reason not to do something that they are uncomfortable with or which may be difficult for them or their dog. The following are common myths and misconceptions:

1. If your dog leaves when you want him to be working the stock he will never want to work stock again.

Most times that a dog leaves when you are working stock are the result of too much pressure from the handler or the situation. It may be the result of trying to force the dog to do something, when you should have helped him instead. If you talk to people who have worked with many dogs, they will tell you that most dogs will have some point where they may not want to work and will leave the stock. Sometimes you will make a correction that results in this response; that doesn't necessarily mean that the correction was too harsh, but it could mean that the correction was too harsh. Forget it and go on. If you forget it, the dog will forget it!

Your dog is going to have to learn to take a lot of pressure if you want to train to an advanced level. As you expect more out of him, you and the sheep will be placing more pressure on him. You want your dog to learn that your correction is for the action and not to take your corrections personally. He should know that you still like him, but that you did not like what he just did.

If your dog leaves the stock, go get the dog, put him on a leash and bring him back to stock. Forget about trying to do the thing that caused the problem. Try to make him happy to come back to work. Then, you can gradually work on the problem again. It is rare that a dog will not go back to work with this approach. It is usually only a problem if you make it a problem and go after the dog telling him that you are mad at him!

2. *If you make a mistake with your dog while training you will ruin him and he will make that mistake forever.*

The only time this is true is if you practice your mistake over and over. That is why it is important to be able to identify problems early and correct them early. If a particular command is a problem, you may have to change to a new word in order to get a different response. This way you discontinue the old word and the old habit associated with it.

Everyone makes mistakes. If you make a mistake once in a while it will not form a habit. Just make sure that you do not practice the same mistake repeatedly! Dogs are usually wonderfully forgiving and are usually more tolerant of our mistakes than we are of theirs!

Don't be so afraid of making a mistake that you do not try things or challenge yourself or your dog. Only by making mistakes will you both be able to learn from them.

3. Your dog should always be happy in his work to learn something.

It is great if your dog can be happy during the training process, but it is not always possible to make every training experience a happy one. Remember when you were in school—some lessons were very difficult but you had to persevere, some days you wished you were not there, and some days it was fun and exciting to learn. But, overall, you continued to learn. Looking back you may have realized that the teacher that had high expectations and standards for you and that you liked the least at the time, actually taught you the most and you appreciate what you learned from them.

A lot of things that you don't enjoy at the beginning will become more rewarding when you have learned to do it. I try to make most training and learning experiences as stress-free and enjoyable as possible for myself and my dog, but realize that there will be times when the training and learning process will include some more difficult and less fun times.

When I am training or working a dog I do not always expect him to be perfect, although I have high expectations for him with regards to his performance. Therefore, my feelings are not hurt and I do not take it personally if he makes a mistake or is not perfect in a particular situation.

4. Always stop a training session on a good note.

It is nice if you can let your dog have some success and end a training session on a good note. However, there may be some days when, if you are trying to stop on a good note, it would be impossible. This may be because you and/or your dog is tired and you may not have enough energy between the two of you to find that good note. If nothing is going right, it may be better to just stop your training session and come back to start again later in the day or tomorrow. Sometimes it is better to just stop than it is to try to stop on a good note!

5. If your dog circles around stock, this will teach him to always circle stock and you will not be able to control him or teach him to drive.

There is a difference between the dog that goes out and around stock and the dog that rings his sheep. The dog that rings his sheep will go out and run in circles around his stock without thought for moving them or including the handler as part of the situation. This may be because the dog has gotten loose and worked stock on his own or has been allowed to do this for too long without moving on in his training or without supervision.

Some people think that the dog that heads sheep when they run past the handler and continues past the handler is ringing his sheep. This often happens with young or inexperienced dogs when they are first starting out. Actually he has been doing the right thing and keeping his sheep from escaping. If the dog cannot learn to control stock when they are passing you and only controls them when they are behind you, he has only learned half of his job!

If a dog is overly keen to go to the head, you will have to teach him to stay behind the stock and put pressure on the sheep from behind. If he goes to the head, put him back in position behind his sheep and start again. This may become a habit quickly, so learn to recognize this and correct it.

6. If you walk with your dog through the middle of the sheep, this will teach him to split sheep and he will always want to do this.

If you allow your dog to run free and to chase sheep, he will learn bad habits, such as splitting or scattering sheep. If you ask your dog to walk through sheep with you, this is okay because you have asked your dog to do this purposely. Dogs that are nervous or panicked around sheep will benefit from walking around and through the middle of the sheep. It is also helpful to make your dog accustomed to this so that you can get across a field full of sheep in order to look at one. This is a common practice. Also, someday you will want to ask this dog to shed and he will need to learn to be comfortable walking through sheep. As long as you have asked your dog to walk through the middle of the sheep and he has not scattered the sheep or split them on his own or because he is wanting to create some fun for himself, this should not be a problem.

7. *Having a dog drag a rope will destroy his confidence.*

A dog dragging a rope will not result in a decrease in confidence or prevent your dog from developing confidence. A rope is only a training aid. Most dogs will not even realize they are dragging a light rope. In fact, when you pick up a rope to help your dog or to provide some guidance for him, you may be helping him to increase his confidence! Sometimes you may have a long rope on your young dog or puppy to help you catch him and then will go to using a shorter rope for more advanced training. It is easier to pick up the rope and show the dog what you want him to do than it is to stand and shout at him and have him be confused about what you want him to do. By showing and helping him, he will gain more confidence than he will if you are shouting at him. When training it is better to have the rope in case you need it, than it is to wish you had it and not have it when you need it.

8. *You shouldn't start your dog in a small pen or work your dog in a small pen because he will learn to work too close to the stock and will not widen out.*

I do not think starting a dog in a small pen has anything to do with whether or not he will eventually learn to widen out. I think of the enclosure as a controlled learning environment where you will be more likely to provide a positive experience for you and your dog. When you start a young dog in a small pen you are using this space to help him learn how to go around the stock, learn to be comfortable going between the fence and the stock, learn to fetch, hold sheep to you and learn to out or back. If he is having problems you are close by and can be there to help him. If out in the open, it is easier to have things get out of control and you may not be able to help him as quickly or as easily. If a dog is running or chasing in a larger area this is not teaching him anything and is very frustrating! Imagine if you were trying to teach a child to read and you put a book on the back of the bicycle and then took off as fast as you can with your child running along behind it and trying to learn how to read. Do you expect that he would be able to become an expert reader quickly?

Some experienced handlers have the experience and ability to make a learning experience happen in a larger area. However, inexperienced handlers may often need a smaller area in which to provide an environment within which both the dog and the handler can learn.

Once you and your dog have become comfortable in a smaller area it is important to be able to move out into a larger area. If you continue to stay in the small area, you will limit both yourself and your dog. If you both want to grow in your abilities and make progress you will have to leave the smaller pen.

9. *If you are having trouble with verbal commands, change to whistles. Whistles don't show emotion or panic like your voice does.*

If you can communicate tension, panic or emotion in your voice, you can also communicate this with a whistle. It will come through, no matter what you do! You may not be as aware of it with your whistle as you are with your voice. It may be harder for other people to detect unless they know your whistles well or have heard you work with whistles at home when you are relaxed. If people are excited or frustrated you can often detect this in their whistles—they may be louder, sharper or sound different than they do when they are relaxed and working at home. So, learn to concentrate, relax and control your voice AND your whistles. Use the tape recorder, as I've suggested in the Chapter on Whistles in this book to determine if your whistles are different when you are under tension.

10. *You should not pat or play with a herding dog.*

This is a common misconception. Patting your dog, talking to your dog and playing with your dog will not influence whether he herds well or not. It actually is beneficial in establishing a good relationship with him. You should be able to make it clear to your dog that there is a difference between when you are playing and when you are working. If you mix play and work together, your dog may fail to develop a good work ethic. A dog with a good work ethic—who knows that he needs to work and stick with it even if it is difficult—will be a better dog than the dog that only wants to play or who will leave and want to go to other people or other dogs instead of working stock. This will depend on how you have raised your dog and what he has learned as part of his puppy training. You want a dog that will be friendly and well adjusted around other people and other dogs, but do not want a dog that seeks their attention to the exclusion of working stock.

11. *The roof of the mouth of a herding dog should be back.*

All a black mouth shows is that a dog has a lot of black pigment. I've never seen a dog run out on the field and right before he gets to the sheep stop and open his mouth. I've never seen the sheep look in a dog's mouth and say 'Oh, black mouth—we better be good; partial black mouth—we can be moderately bad; or pink mouth—we can be really bad.' The black mouth may be important because it usually goes with black pigment around the eyes and a decreased probability of development of skin cancer or hypersensitivity associated with exposure to the sun.

12. *A dog with a lot of white, a red dog, or a merle dog will be a weaker dog than a black and white dog.*

I believe that stock is more likely to notice a dog that is black or has some white, but not a lot of white. It may be because this provides some contrast. A light dog or dogs with more white or of different colors will commonly have to come closer to the stock before they are noticed. But, this is not always the case. If they come closer to the stock, they may startle the stock or may be more likely to be challenged. If they are repeatedly challenged and do not develop the confidence to handle this, they may become even less confident in doing their job and appear to be weak. It is easy to find fault with a dog based on his color. There have been some great dogs of all colors!

Concluding Remarks

As you are around herding people, you will hear a lot of myths and misconception. Don't just accept what people say without applying some critical thought. If you hear someone make a statement like those above, see if they can explain to you why they are saying this. Many generalizations will have a basis in truth and in a particular situation, but then will be applied more broadly than or in situations in which they are not pertinent. Make your own judgments based on sound principles and observations.

Bob Vest with his champion Australian Shepherd dog, Lynn

The Traveling Herding Teacher

How This Book Came About

I had the opportunity to attend multiple clinics with Bob Vest when I first started learning about herding when I lived in the United States. I always learned a lot from Bob and appreciated his insights into learning and thoughts about how dogs and stock think and why they react in certain ways. I kept in touch with Bob when I moved to the United Kingdom, where I work as a clinical pathologist and farm part time. Over the last 17 years, I have had the opportunity to farm with my late husband, John Angus MacLeod, a renowned sheep dog trialist and stockman. Over the years John Angus and I had a flock of around 1,500 ewes with grazing on one of the highest continually-grazed hills in Scotland (Ben Ghlas and Ben Lawers, near Killin, Perthshire). I continue to farm with my new husband, Iain Kelly, a dedicated shepherd and stockman, now cut down to approximately 500 ewes due to loss of a grazing lease we previously held. I have had the opportunity to trial throughout Scotland, as well as participate in or view trials in England, Wales, Ireland and continental Europe. I have enjoyed judging sheep dog trials in Scotland, Sweden, and Italy and was honored to judge the Scottish National Sheep Dog Trial with Neil McVicar in 2011.

I have given a lot of thought to training techniques and working styles with various types of dogs and handlers. It is always interesting to watch a variety of dogs and handlers. It has been a real experience to work dogs on the hill and to be able to be part of the culture of shepherding and farming that still exists in the hills where the

Border Collie was developed. Over the years, I read a variety of books published by sheep dog enthusiasts and trainers. I felt that Bob's techniques deserved to be published, as well. I invited him to come over to visit in order to develop this book. He would do the talking and I would type and take notes, taking care of the organization and writing down things in this venture. So, with some urging from Rachel, Bob finally took a plan, a train, and a car and landed on my doorstep in Scotland. We took some breaks to enjoy dog training and the local countryside, but spent two weeks, with many hours of work daily to develop the first draft of this book.

When Bob went back to the United States we exchanged revisions by e-mail. Bob was to find an illustrator for this book, but passed away before this could be accomplished. After his death, this manuscript lay in my drawer for several years before I decided to pick it up again and finish it.

It is a labor of love and with great respect that I have reviewed the material and taken it for publication. It is an honor to have known Bob Vest and I hope that this book will help those that knew him remember his work and those that did not have the opportunity to know Bob, to benefit from his great expertise and experience.

Kathleen Freeman Kelly

www.ingramcontent.com/pod-product-compliance
Lightning Source LLC
Chambersburg PA
CBHW081353230426
43667CB00017B/2820